# App Protection and Privacy Mastery

## How to Secure Mobile Apps, Control Permissions, and Stop Apps From Tracking Your Data

*By Joe Correa*

Published by Live Stronger Faster



This book is for educational and informational purposes only. The author and publisher are not engaged in rendering legal, financial, or other professional advice. Readers should consult a qualified professional before making any financial decisions.

First Edition

# Table of Contents

# Introduction

Welcome to *App Protection and Privacy Mastery*, the second book in the *Mobile Security & App Protection Academy: The Complete 10-in-1 Cybersecurity Collection*. In today's digital world, mobile applications have become deeply integrated into nearly every aspect of daily life. From communication and banking to shopping, entertainment, healthcare, transportation, education, and work, apps have transformed smartphones into powerful tools that connect us to virtually every service imaginable. While these technologies provide tremendous convenience and productivity, they also introduce significant privacy and security risks that many users do not fully understand. Every app installed on a mobile device has the potential to access personal information, track behavior, collect data, share information with third parties, and create security vulnerabilities that can expose users to cybercriminals, advertisers, data brokers, and even invasive surveillance practices.

Most people assume that downloading an app from an official app store automatically guarantees safety and privacy. Unfortunately, that assumption is often incorrect. While major app stores do perform security reviews and remove many malicious applications, countless apps continue to collect excessive amounts of personal information. Some applications request permissions that far exceed what is necessary for their intended functionality. Others gather detailed information about users' habits, interests, locations, contacts, browsing patterns, and purchasing behaviors. In many cases, users unknowingly grant access to this information simply by accepting lengthy terms of service agreements without understanding what they are authorizing. This creates a digital environment where personal data becomes a valuable commodity that can be collected, analyzed, sold, and used in ways users never intended.

The purpose of this book is to help you regain control over your digital privacy. Rather than accepting app tracking and data collection as unavoidable aspects of modern technology, you will learn practical strategies for protecting yourself while still enjoying the benefits that mobile applications provide. Privacy is not about hiding wrongdoing. Privacy is about maintaining control over your personal information, protecting your identity, safeguarding your finances, and preserving your freedom to make choices without constant monitoring. Understanding how apps operate behind the scenes empowers you to make informed decisions about which applications deserve access to your device and which ones should be avoided altogether.

One of the most important concepts you will explore throughout this book is the role of app permissions. Permissions are the gateways that allow applications to access various functions and data stored on your device. These may include your camera, microphone, contacts, location, photos, messages, storage, calendar, Bluetooth connections, and more. While many permissions are legitimate and necessary for certain features to function properly, others may be excessive or unnecessary. A flashlight app, for example, generally does not need access to your contacts. A calculator app should not require location tracking. Understanding how permissions work enables users to identify red flags and reduce unnecessary exposure of personal information.

Another major topic covered in this book is mobile app tracking. Many apps use sophisticated technologies to monitor user behavior across multiple platforms and services. Advertisers and data brokers rely on tracking systems to build detailed profiles that can reveal interests, habits, spending patterns, travel behavior, social relationships, and even political preferences. While personalized advertising may seem harmless on the surface, the amount of information collected can be extensive. By learning how tracking systems operate, readers will gain valuable insight into the hidden mechanisms that fuel the modern data economy and discover practical methods for limiting unwanted surveillance.

In recent years, privacy concerns have become increasingly important as cybersecurity threats continue to evolve. Data breaches have exposed billions of user records worldwide. Cybercriminals constantly seek opportunities to exploit personal information for identity theft, financial fraud, phishing attacks, account takeovers, and social engineering schemes. The more information that apps collect and store, the more valuable those databases become to attackers. A single compromised application can expose usernames, passwords, addresses, phone numbers, financial information, and other sensitive details. Protecting privacy is therefore not only a matter of personal preference but also a critical component of overall cybersecurity.

As mobile technology becomes more advanced, so do the methods used to collect data. Modern applications can gather information through GPS sensors, motion sensors, wireless networks, Bluetooth connections, cookies, advertising identifiers, device fingerprints, and numerous other techniques. Some forms of data collection occur directly through permissions granted by users, while others happen behind the scenes through complex analytics systems embedded within applications. This book will demystify these technologies and explain them in straightforward language so that readers can understand how information flows from their devices to third parties.

Throughout this book, you will discover that privacy protection does not require advanced technical expertise. Many effective security measures can be implemented using simple settings that already exist on most smartphones. Small adjustments to permission settings, privacy controls, app configurations, and browsing habits can dramatically reduce data exposure. By developing a proactive mindset and learning how to evaluate applications critically, users can significantly improve their security posture without sacrificing convenience or functionality.

You will also learn how different mobile operating systems approach privacy and security. Android and iOS each provide unique tools and controls that allow users to manage permissions, restrict tracking, review app behavior, and protect sensitive information. Understanding the strengths and limitations of each platform enables users to take full advantage of available security features. Whether you use an Android smartphone, an iPhone, or multiple devices, the concepts presented in this book will help you build stronger privacy habits and make more informed decisions.

Another critical aspect of app protection involves evaluating the trustworthiness of developers and software providers. Not all applications are created equal. Some companies invest heavily in user privacy and transparent security practices, while others prioritize aggressive data collection and monetization strategies. Learning how to research app developers, review privacy policies, interpret permission requests, and identify warning signs can help users avoid risky applications before they ever reach their devices. Prevention is often far more effective than responding to a security incident after it occurs.

The rise of artificial intelligence, machine learning, and advanced analytics has also transformed how organizations collect and use personal information. Modern systems can process enormous volumes of data to identify patterns, predict behaviors, and influence decision-making. While these technologies offer significant benefits, they also raise important privacy questions. Understanding how your data contributes to these systems helps you make informed choices about what information you share and with whom. This awareness is becoming increasingly important as digital ecosystems continue to expand and integrate into everyday life.

This book is designed for readers of all experience levels. Whether you are a complete beginner seeking to improve your mobile security or a technology enthusiast looking to deepen your understanding of privacy protection, the material has been structured to provide practical knowledge that can be applied immediately. Each chapter builds upon foundational concepts while introducing new techniques and strategies that strengthen your overall cybersecurity awareness. The goal is not simply to provide information but to help you develop habits that support long-term digital safety.

By the end of this book, you will possess a comprehensive understanding of how mobile applications collect data, how permissions work, how tracking technologies operate, and how to minimize unnecessary exposure of personal information. More importantly, you will gain the confidence to take control of your digital environment rather than allowing technology companies, advertisers, or cybercriminals to dictate how your information is used. In a world where personal data has become one of the most valuable resources on the planet, knowledge is one of the most effective forms of protection.

The journey toward stronger privacy and app security begins with awareness. Every permission granted, every app installed, and every piece of information shared contributes to your digital footprint. The choices you make today can have long-term implications for your privacy, security, finances, and personal freedom. As you move through the chapters ahead, you will learn how to make those choices wisely, confidently, and strategically. Welcome to *App Protection and Privacy*

*Mastery*. Your path toward greater digital control, stronger privacy, and enhanced mobile security starts now.

*Chapter 1*

# Understanding Mobile Apps, Privacy, and Data Collection

Mobile applications have become one of the most important technologies in modern life. Millions of people rely on apps every day to communicate with friends and family, manage finances, shop online, navigate unfamiliar locations, monitor health, consume entertainment, and perform countless other activities. While these applications provide tremendous convenience, they also create opportunities for companies and cybercriminals to collect, analyze, and potentially misuse personal information. Understanding how mobile apps operate and how they collect data is the foundation of protecting your privacy and securing your digital life.

Every mobile application is designed to perform a specific function. Some apps help users send messages, others stream videos, provide banking services, or manage work projects. To perform these functions, apps often require access to information stored on your device or generated through your activities. This information may include your location, contacts, photographs, browsing history, device identifiers, microphone recordings, camera access, and much more. While some data collection is necessary for functionality, many applications collect significantly more information than they actually need.

One of the first concepts every mobile user must understand is that personal data has become one of the world's most valuable commodities. Large technology companies generate billions of dollars annually by collecting information about users and using it to improve advertising effectiveness. Every click, search, purchase, location visit, and interaction helps create a detailed profile that advertisers can use to target products and services. In many cases, users unknowingly provide this information simply by using free applications.

The business model behind many free apps is not actually the application itself. Instead, the user's data becomes the product. When an application is offered without charge, the developer often generates revenue through advertising networks, analytics services, partnerships, or data-sharing arrangements. This does not necessarily mean every free app is dangerous, but it does mean users should carefully consider what information they are providing in exchange for free access.

Mobile apps collect information through various methods. One common method involves direct user input. Whenever you create an account, complete a profile, upload photos, enter payment information, or communicate through an application, you are providing data directly to the app provider. Another method involves automatic collection. Applications can gather information about your device model, operating system version, network connections, usage patterns, battery status, and location without requiring manual input.

Many users are surprised to learn how much information can be collected from location services alone. Modern smartphones continuously generate location data through GPS signals, Wi-Fi networks, Bluetooth connections, and cellular towers. Applications that have location permissions can potentially track where users live, work, shop, exercise, travel, and socialize. Over time, these location records can reveal highly detailed behavioral patterns. For this reason, location permissions should always be granted carefully and only when necessary.

Device identifiers represent another important category of collected information. Every smartphone contains unique identifiers that help applications recognize individual devices. Advertising networks frequently use these identifiers to track users across multiple apps and websites. Even if users do not provide their names directly, device identifiers can still be linked to extensive behavioral profiles. Understanding how these identifiers work helps users appreciate why privacy settings and tracking restrictions are so important.

Another major source of data collection comes from app analytics systems. Developers use analytics platforms to understand how people interact with their applications. These systems can measure how often users open an app, which features they use, how long they spend on specific screens, and where they encounter difficulties. While analytics can help improve user experiences, they can also contribute to extensive tracking if implemented without adequate privacy protections.

Permissions play a central role in mobile privacy. Permissions are requests that allow applications to access specific device functions or information. Common permissions include access to cameras, microphones, contacts, calendars, storage, photos, location services, and notifications. When users install an application, they often encounter permission requests that seem routine. However, each permission represents a potential privacy decision that should be evaluated carefully.

One useful principle is the concept of least privilege. This cybersecurity principle states that applications should only receive the minimum permissions necessary to perform their intended functions. For example, a weather application may need location access to provide local forecasts, but it probably does not need access to contacts or microphone recordings. Evaluating permissions through this lens helps users identify potentially excessive requests.

Privacy policies are another important aspect of understanding app behavior. Most applications publish privacy policies describing how they collect, store, use, and share information. Unfortunately, these documents are often lengthy and written in complex legal language. While few users read privacy policies in full, learning to review key sections can provide valuable insights. Important areas include data collection practices, third-party sharing arrangements, data retention policies, and user rights regarding information access or deletion.

Third-party software development kits, often called SDKs, contribute significantly to mobile tracking. Many app developers integrate external services that provide advertising, analytics, social media integration, payment processing, or other functionality. These third-party components may collect information independently from the primary application. As a result, user data may be shared with multiple organizations even when interacting with a single app.

Cloud computing has further expanded the scope of mobile data collection. Information generated on smartphones is often transmitted to remote servers where it can be stored, processed, analyzed, and shared. Cloud storage provides convenience and accessibility but also introduces security considerations. Users should understand where their information is stored, who has access to it, and how it is protected.

Cybercriminals frequently target mobile applications because of the valuable information they contain. Attackers may exploit software vulnerabilities, steal login credentials, distribute malicious applications, or launch phishing attacks designed to compromise user accounts. The more information collected and stored by an application, the more attractive it becomes as a target. This reinforces the importance of minimizing unnecessary data exposure.

Modern operating systems have introduced numerous privacy enhancements to address these concerns. Android and iOS now provide permission management systems, app privacy reports, tracking controls, and security dashboards that help users understand how applications access information. Learning to use these tools effectively is one of the simplest and most powerful steps users can take to improve mobile privacy.

Digital privacy should not be viewed as an all-or-nothing concept. Most people cannot completely eliminate data collection from their digital lives. Instead, privacy protection involves making informed choices that reduce unnecessary exposure while preserving convenience and functionality. The goal is not perfection but awareness and control.

As technology continues evolving, privacy challenges will become increasingly complex. Artificial intelligence systems, biometric authentication, wearable devices, and interconnected digital ecosystems create new opportunities for data collection and analysis. Building a strong understanding of privacy fundamentals today prepares users to navigate these future challenges with confidence and awareness.

Ultimately, mobile security begins with knowledge. Users who understand how applications collect information, why companies seek data, how permissions function, and what risks exist are far better equipped to protect themselves. The lessons introduced in this chapter provide the foundation for all subsequent topics in this book. As you continue your journey through mobile privacy and app protection, remember that every informed decision contributes to a safer and more secure digital experience.

### *Michael watched a documentary about digital privacy*

Michael considered himself fairly knowledgeable about technology. At forty-two years old, he owned a successful landscaping company and used his smartphone constantly throughout the day. He managed appointments, communicated with clients, accepted payments, tracked employee schedules, and advertised his business through social media. His phone had become an essential part of both his professional and personal life.

One evening, Michael watched a documentary about digital privacy. The program described how apps collected personal information and built detailed profiles of users. At first, he dismissed the concerns. He believed he had nothing to hide and assumed the information being collected was harmless. However, one segment captured his attention. The documentary demonstrated how location data could reveal a person's daily routine, workplace, favorite restaurants, gym visits, and even social relationships.

Curious, Michael opened the settings menu on his smartphone and reviewed his app permissions for the first time. He was shocked by what he found. Several applications had continuous access to his location. A simple flashlight app had permission to access storage and contacts. A game he had not played in months still possessed multiple permissions. Many apps requested access to information that seemed unrelated to their intended purpose.

The discovery made Michael uncomfortable. He realized he had accepted nearly every permission request without question. Over the years, he had installed hundreds of applications, trusting that they would only access what was necessary. Now he began to wonder how much information was being collected and where it was being sent.

The following weekend, Michael decided to investigate further. He researched mobile privacy and learned about advertising identifiers, analytics systems, third-party tracking technologies, and data brokers. The more he learned, the more he understood that his smartphone generated a continuous stream of information. Every location visit, app interaction, and online search contributed to a growing digital profile.

One particularly eye-opening experience occurred when Michael noticed advertisements appearing on multiple platforms shortly after discussing a product with a friend. Although he could not determine exactly why the ads appeared, the timing reinforced his growing awareness of how sophisticated digital marketing had become. He realized that even seemingly small pieces of information could be combined to create highly accurate predictions about user interests and behaviors.

Determined to improve his privacy, Michael began making changes. He reviewed every application installed on his phone and removed those he no longer used. He disabled unnecessary permissions and restricted location access whenever possible. He reset advertising identifiers and explored privacy settings that he had never previously noticed. While the process took several hours, he felt a growing sense of control as he worked through each setting.

As weeks passed, Michael developed new habits. Before installing applications, he researched developers and read reviews carefully. He paid attention to permission requests and questioned whether they were reasonable. Instead of automatically granting access, he evaluated each request based on necessity. These small changes quickly became routine.

One day, Michael's younger sister Sarah called him. She had recently received a suspicious message claiming that one of her accounts had been compromised. Unsure what to do, she asked for advice. Drawing upon everything he had learned, Michael helped her verify the legitimacy of the message and secure her account. More importantly, he explained how privacy awareness could help prevent future problems.

Their conversation inspired Michael to share his knowledge with employees at his company. During a team meeting, he spent a few minutes discussing smartphone security and privacy practices. To his surprise, many employees admitted they had never reviewed their permissions or privacy settings. Several expressed interest in learning more about protecting personal information.

Over time, Michael realized that privacy was not about fear or paranoia. It was about understanding technology and making informed decisions. He still used social media, banking apps, navigation services, and entertainment platforms. The difference was that he now understood the tradeoffs involved and actively managed the information he shared.

Months later, Michael reflected on how much his perspective had changed. What began as curiosity after watching a documentary had evolved into a comprehensive understanding of mobile privacy. He no longer viewed data collection as an abstract concept. He recognized it as a fundamental aspect of modern technology that required attention and responsibility.

Most importantly, Michael discovered that meaningful privacy improvements did not require advanced technical skills. Small, practical actions had significantly reduced unnecessary data exposure. By learning how applications operated and taking control of his settings, he had strengthened both his privacy and security.

His experience demonstrated an important lesson. In a world increasingly driven by data, awareness is one of the most powerful tools available. Every user has the ability to make smarter decisions, protect personal information, and reduce digital risks. The journey begins with understanding how mobile apps collect data and recognizing that privacy is not something that happens automatically—it is something that must be actively managed and protected.

*Chapter 2*

# App Permissions Explained – Taking Control of What Apps Can Access

One of the most powerful tools available for protecting your privacy and securing your mobile device is understanding app permissions. Every mobile application requires certain permissions to perform its intended functions. Permissions act as security checkpoints that determine what information and device features an app can access. While many permissions are legitimate and necessary, others may grant applications access to sensitive information that is not essential for their operation. Learning how permissions work allows users to take control of their digital privacy and reduce unnecessary exposure of personal data.

When smartphones first became popular, many users simply installed applications and accepted all permission requests without question. Developers often presented long lists of requested permissions during installation, and users would approve them to quickly begin using the app. As mobile technology evolved, operating systems recognized the privacy risks associated with this approach. Today, modern platforms such as Android and iOS provide much more granular permission controls, allowing users to decide exactly what information applications can access and when that access is granted.

At its core, a permission is simply a request made by an application to access a specific feature, service, or category of information on your device. Examples include access to your camera, microphone, location, contacts, calendar, storage, photos, Bluetooth connections, motion sensors, and notifications. When an app requests permission, it is essentially asking for authorization to interact with that portion of your device or data.

The first category of permissions many users encounter involves location services. Location access is among the most sensitive permissions because it can reveal where you live, work, travel, shop, exercise, and spend your free time. Modern smartphones can determine location through GPS satellites, Wi-Fi networks, cellular towers, and Bluetooth signals. Applications that receive location permissions can often collect extremely detailed movement histories. While navigation apps legitimately require location access, many other apps request it for advertising, analytics, or behavioral tracking purposes. Users should carefully evaluate whether location access is truly necessary before granting permission.

Modern operating systems typically provide several location options. Users may choose to allow location access all the time, only while using the app, ask every time, or deny access entirely. From a privacy perspective, granting access only while actively using an app is often the safest choice. This minimizes background tracking and limits the amount of location information available to developers and third parties.

Camera permissions represent another important area of privacy management. Applications that access your camera can capture photos and videos, scan documents, participate in video calls, or support augmented reality experiences. While camera access is essential for many legitimate purposes, users should be cautious when applications unrelated to photography or communication request this permission. A simple note-taking app or puzzle game generally has little reason to access your camera.

Microphone permissions deserve similar attention. Smartphones contain highly sensitive microphones capable of recording conversations, environmental sounds, and voice commands. Communication platforms, voice assistants, and recording applications naturally require microphone access. However, users should review microphone permissions regularly to ensure only trusted applications maintain access. Limiting microphone permissions reduces opportunities for unauthorized audio collection and helps preserve personal privacy.

Contact permissions allow applications to view information stored in your address book. This may include names, phone numbers, email addresses, physical addresses, and notes associated with contacts. Messaging apps often require contact access to help users find friends and family already using the service. However, granting contact permissions also means sharing information about other people who may not have consented to that disclosure. Users should carefully consider whether the benefits outweigh the privacy implications before granting contact access.

Photo and storage permissions provide applications access to images, videos, documents, and files stored on a device. Historically, many apps requested broad access to entire photo libraries. Newer privacy features now allow users to share only selected images with specific applications. This represents a significant improvement because it prevents apps from viewing unrelated personal photos and documents. Whenever possible, users should utilize limited-access options rather than granting unrestricted file access.

Calendar permissions enable applications to read and modify scheduling information. Productivity tools may use this access to create appointments, send reminders, or coordinate meetings. However, calendar data can reveal substantial information about a person's daily activities, business relationships, travel plans, and routines. As with all permissions, access should be granted only when there is a clear functional need.

Bluetooth permissions have become increasingly important in recent years. Bluetooth technology allows smartphones to connect with wireless accessories, smart home devices, wearable technology, and vehicle systems. Some applications request Bluetooth access for legitimate connectivity purposes, while others may use Bluetooth signals to estimate location or track nearby devices. Understanding why an application requests Bluetooth access helps users make informed decisions.

Notification permissions might appear harmless, but they can significantly impact privacy and security. Notifications often contain previews of messages, emails, financial alerts, and authentication codes. Some applications use notifications responsibly, while others may overwhelm users with marketing content or unnecessary alerts. Managing notification permissions improves both privacy and overall user experience.

Motion and fitness permissions allow applications to access information from device sensors such as accelerometers and gyroscopes. These sensors can detect movement patterns, exercise activities, and physical behavior. Fitness trackers naturally rely on such information, but users should be aware that motion data can sometimes reveal more about their habits and routines than expected.

One of the most valuable habits users can develop is performing regular permission audits. A permission audit involves reviewing all installed applications and examining which permissions they currently possess. During this process, users should ask several questions. Does this permission support the app's primary purpose? Is the developer trustworthy? Would the application still function adequately without this permission? If the answer suggests the permission is unnecessary, it should be revoked.

The principle of least privilege remains one of the most effective strategies for permission management. Applications should receive only the minimum access required to perform their intended functions. This principle reduces potential damage if an app becomes compromised, behaves unexpectedly, or shares information with third parties. By limiting permissions, users create additional layers of protection around sensitive data.

Operating systems continue introducing new privacy features that enhance permission control. Temporary permissions, one-time access requests, privacy dashboards, permission usage reports, and app activity indicators provide greater transparency than ever before. Users who take advantage of these tools gain valuable insight into how applications interact with their devices.

Another important consideration involves permission fatigue. Users often encounter so many permission requests that they begin approving them automatically without careful evaluation. Cybercriminals and unethical developers sometimes exploit this tendency by requesting excessive permissions in the hope that users will simply click "Allow." Developing a habit of pausing and evaluating each request can significantly improve privacy protection.

Enterprise environments also rely heavily on permission management. Organizations that allow employees to use smartphones for work often implement policies governing app permissions and device security. Sensitive corporate information can be exposed if applications receive excessive access. Understanding permission management therefore benefits both personal and professional cybersecurity efforts.

As technology continues advancing, permission systems will likely become even more sophisticated. Artificial intelligence, augmented reality, wearable devices, smart homes, and interconnected ecosystems will create new categories of permissions and privacy considerations. Building strong permission management habits today prepares users for future developments and helps ensure ongoing control over personal information.

Ultimately, app permissions represent one of the most direct ways users can influence their digital privacy. Every permission granted creates a pathway through which information can flow. By understanding what permissions do, evaluating requests critically, and conducting regular audits, users can dramatically reduce unnecessary data exposure while maintaining the functionality they need. Taking control of permissions is not about restricting technology—it is about ensuring technology serves your interests rather than compromising your privacy.

***Emma attended a cybersecurity workshop***

Emma loved trying new mobile applications. At thirty-five years old, she considered herself an enthusiastic technology user. Her smartphone contained apps for fitness tracking, meal planning, social networking, budgeting, shopping, travel, photography, language learning, and countless other activities. Whenever friends recommended a useful app, she usually downloaded it immediately.

One afternoon, Emma attended a cybersecurity workshop organized by her employer. The presenter discussed mobile privacy and demonstrated how permissions allowed applications to access sensitive information. During the presentation, participants were encouraged to review the permissions granted to their installed apps.

Emma opened her settings menu and began scrolling through the list. What she discovered surprised her. A flashlight application had access to her location. A photo editing app had permission to use her microphone. Several shopping apps could access her contacts. One simple game had access to storage, location services, and Bluetooth. She realized she had never paid attention to permission requests during installation.

The workshop instructor explained that many applications request more permissions than they actually need. Sometimes developers sought additional data for analytics or advertising purposes. In other cases, permissions were requested because developers used third-party software components that automatically collected information. The instructor emphasized that users should understand why permissions were being requested rather than approving everything automatically.

Motivated by what she learned, Emma spent the weekend conducting a full permission audit of her smartphone. She reviewed each application individually and asked herself whether the permissions made sense. If an app's purpose did not justify the requested access, she revoked the permission.

The process was eye-opening. She discovered dozens of permissions that served little apparent purpose. Some apps continued functioning perfectly after permissions were removed. Others requested access again when specific features were used, allowing Emma to make more informed decisions based on actual needs rather than assumptions.

One particular discovery caught her attention. A weather app had continuous location access enabled, allowing it to track her movements throughout the day. Emma changed the setting so location was only available while actively using the app. The weather forecasts continued working normally, but unnecessary background tracking stopped.

Encouraged by her success, Emma began sharing what she learned with friends and family. During a family gathering, she helped her parents review permissions on their smartphones.

Her father was shocked to discover that several applications could access his contacts and location despite having no obvious need for either. Together, they adjusted settings and improved privacy protections.

Several months later, Emma noticed a change in how she approached technology. Rather than blindly accepting permission requests, she evaluated them carefully. When a new app requested access to her microphone, she asked herself whether voice functionality was genuinely necessary. When an application requested location tracking, she considered whether the benefit justified the privacy tradeoff.

This new mindset extended beyond permissions. Emma became more aware of privacy settings, app reputations, developer transparency, and data collection practices. She no longer viewed cybersecurity as something only experts needed to understand. Instead, she recognized that small, everyday decisions could significantly influence privacy outcomes.

One evening, a colleague mentioned concerns about targeted advertisements appearing after discussing certain topics. The conversation reminded Emma of her own journey. She explained how app permissions, tracking technologies, and data collection systems worked together to build behavioral profiles. Her colleague listened with interest and later thanked her for helping him understand the importance of reviewing privacy settings.

As the years passed, Emma continued refining her digital habits. She periodically reviewed permissions, removed unused applications, and stayed informed about new privacy features introduced by smartphone manufacturers. These practices became routine, requiring little effort while providing substantial benefits.

Looking back, Emma realized that her greatest lesson was not about technology itself. It was about awareness. Permissions represented choices. Every request provided an opportunity to decide what information would be shared and under what conditions. By understanding those choices, she gained greater control over her digital life.

Her experience demonstrated a simple but powerful truth: privacy is rarely lost through a single dramatic event. More often, it is gradually surrendered through countless small decisions made without consideration. By learning to evaluate permissions thoughtfully, Emma transformed those decisions into opportunities for protection, empowerment, and control.

The lesson remained with her every time she installed a new app. A permission request was no longer a minor inconvenience to dismiss quickly. It was a moment to pause, think, and decide whether access was truly necessary. That simple habit became one of the most effective privacy protections she would ever adopt.

*Chapter 3*

# How Mobile Apps Track You and What You Can Do About It

One of the most important realities of modern mobile technology is that many applications are designed not only to provide useful services but also to collect information about user behavior. Every day, billions of smartphone users generate enormous amounts of data through app usage, internet browsing, purchases, social interactions, location updates, and countless other digital activities. This information has become one of the most valuable resources in the digital economy. Understanding how mobile apps track users is essential for anyone seeking to protect their privacy and maintain control over personal information.

Many people assume that tracking only occurs when they are actively using an application. In reality, tracking can occur before, during, and after app usage. Some applications continue collecting information in the background, even when users are not actively interacting with them. Depending on the permissions granted and the design of the app, tracking may include location data, browsing activity, device information, purchasing behavior, app usage statistics, social interactions, and more.

The primary reason most companies track users is to gather information that can be used to improve products, personalize experiences, increase advertising effectiveness, and generate revenue. Data allows organizations to better understand user behavior and predict future actions. While some tracking serves legitimate business purposes, excessive or poorly disclosed tracking practices can create significant privacy concerns.

One of the most common tracking methods involves advertising identifiers. Both Android and iOS devices generate unique advertising IDs that help advertisers recognize individual devices across multiple applications. These identifiers allow advertising networks to observe how users interact with apps, websites, advertisements, and digital content. Over time, these interactions help create detailed profiles describing interests, preferences, shopping habits, and behavioral patterns.

Advertising identifiers are particularly valuable because they allow companies to connect information collected from multiple sources. For example, an advertiser may observe that a user frequently visits fitness websites, uses workout applications, purchases sports equipment, and watches health-related videos. These activities can be combined into a profile that identifies the user as someone interested in health and fitness products. Advertisers can then deliver highly targeted advertisements based on those interests.

Another common tracking method involves cookies and similar technologies. While cookies are often associated with web browsers, many mobile applications use similar systems to remember user preferences, maintain login sessions, and track activity across digital platforms. These technologies can store identifiers and other information that help companies recognize returning users and monitor behavior over time.

Device fingerprinting represents a more advanced form of tracking. Unlike advertising identifiers, which can often be reset or restricted, device fingerprinting attempts to identify users based on unique combinations of device characteristics. Information such as screen size, operating system version, language settings, installed fonts, network configurations, and hardware details can be combined to create a unique digital fingerprint. Even when traditional tracking methods are limited, fingerprinting may still allow companies to recognize users across different sessions.

Location tracking remains one of the most sensitive forms of data collection. Smartphones continuously interact with GPS satellites, cellular networks, Wi-Fi access points, and Bluetooth devices. These interactions allow apps to estimate user locations with remarkable accuracy. Location data can reveal where people live, work, shop, attend school, exercise, worship, and spend leisure time. Over weeks, months, and years, location histories can provide detailed insights into a person's lifestyle, relationships, habits, and routines.

Social media applications often rely heavily on behavioral tracking. Every post viewed, photo liked, video watched, comment written, and account followed contributes to a growing behavioral profile. Machine learning systems analyze these interactions to determine interests and predict future engagement. While users often appreciate personalized content recommendations, they may not realize how much information is being collected and analyzed behind the scenes.

Many mobile applications also utilize third-party tracking systems. Developers frequently integrate external software development kits (SDKs) provided by advertising companies, analytics providers, social media platforms, and other organizations. These third-party components may collect information independently of the primary application. As a result, a single app may share data with numerous external entities without users fully understanding the scope of that sharing.

Cross-app tracking has become a major privacy concern in recent years. Cross-app tracking occurs when information collected in one application is combined with data gathered from other apps. This allows companies to build comprehensive user profiles that extend far beyond any single platform. For example, shopping habits observed in one app may be combined with social media activity, location data, and browsing history collected elsewhere.

Artificial intelligence and machine learning have significantly enhanced tracking capabilities. Modern systems can analyze enormous volumes of data to identify patterns that humans might never recognize. These systems can predict interests, estimate purchasing intentions, assess preferences, and generate highly personalized recommendations. While these technologies offer benefits, they also increase the amount of personal information being processed and analyzed.

The good news is that users have more privacy tools available than ever before. One of the simplest and most effective steps involves reviewing app permissions regularly. Limiting access to location data, contacts, microphones, cameras, and other sensitive information reduces the amount of data available for tracking. Permissions should only be granted when they support a legitimate function that users genuinely need.

Advertising tracking controls provide another important layer of protection. Both Android and iOS allow users to limit ad tracking, reset advertising identifiers, and restrict personalized advertising. While these measures do not eliminate all forms of tracking, they reduce the ability of advertisers to build detailed behavioral profiles based on advertising identifiers.

Privacy-focused browsers can also help reduce tracking activity. Many modern browsers include built-in protections against trackers, fingerprinting attempts, third-party cookies, and malicious scripts. Using privacy-enhancing browsers helps limit the amount of information collected during internet browsing activities.

Virtual private networks, commonly known as VPNs, offer additional protection by encrypting internet traffic and masking IP addresses. Although VPNs do not prevent all forms of tracking, they make it more difficult for certain organizations to monitor online activities and associate them with specific locations or network connections.

Users should also be cautious when creating accounts. Many applications request information that is not strictly necessary for functionality. Providing only essential information reduces the amount of personal data available for collection and analysis. Whenever possible, users should avoid oversharing profile details, demographic information, and optional personal data.

Regularly deleting unused applications is another valuable privacy habit. Every installed app represents a potential source of tracking, data collection, and security risk. Removing apps that no longer serve a purpose reduces the number of entities with access to personal information and decreases the overall attack surface of a device.

Privacy reports and security dashboards provided by modern operating systems offer valuable insights into app behavior. These tools allow users to review which applications access sensitive information, how frequently permissions are used, and whether unusual activity is occurring. Monitoring these reports helps users identify potential concerns before they become serious problems.

Education remains one of the most effective defenses against excessive tracking. Users who understand how tracking technologies operate are far more likely to recognize privacy risks and make informed decisions. Awareness transforms users from passive participants into active managers of their digital lives.

The reality is that complete anonymity is difficult to achieve in today's interconnected world. However, users do not need to eliminate all tracking to significantly improve privacy. Small actions such as managing permissions, limiting ad tracking, using privacy-focused tools, and reviewing app behavior can substantially reduce data exposure. The goal is not perfection but control. By understanding how apps track users and taking proactive steps to limit unnecessary data collection, individuals can enjoy the benefits of modern technology while maintaining greater privacy and security.

### *Daniel noticed something unusual*

Daniel considered himself a fairly typical smartphone user. He checked social media throughout the day, used navigation apps when driving, streamed music during workouts, and frequently shopped online. Technology made life easier, and he rarely thought much about what happened behind the scenes.

One Saturday morning, Daniel met his longtime friend Alex for coffee. During their conversation, Alex mentioned a recent privacy documentary he had watched. The film explained how mobile apps collected data and built detailed profiles of users. Daniel listened politely but remained skeptical.

"I don't think companies really know that much about me," Daniel said.

Alex smiled. "You might be surprised."

Later that evening, curiosity got the better of him. Daniel watched the documentary himself. The program demonstrated how advertisers tracked user activity across multiple apps, collected location histories, and analyzed behavioral patterns. One segment showed how seemingly unrelated pieces of information could be combined to reveal a person's routines, interests, and future intentions.

The next morning, Daniel noticed something unusual. After researching hiking equipment online, advertisements for backpacks, boots, camping gear, and outdoor clothing appeared throughout multiple apps. He had seen targeted ads before, but now he began paying closer attention. The advertisements seemed increasingly relevant to his recent activities.

Curious, he decided to investigate further. He began reading articles about mobile tracking and discovered concepts such as advertising identifiers, device fingerprinting, third-party analytics, and cross-app tracking. The more he learned, the more he realized that modern tracking systems were far more sophisticated than he had imagined.

One evening, Daniel reviewed the privacy settings on his smartphone. He found an option related to advertising personalization and learned that his device maintained a unique advertising identifier. He also discovered several permissions that allowed apps to collect location data continuously.

The realization was unsettling. Daniel understood that companies were not necessarily monitoring him personally. Instead, automated systems were collecting and analyzing information on a massive scale. His data was simply one part of a much larger ecosystem.

Rather than becoming fearful, Daniel decided to become proactive. He adjusted location permissions so apps could only access his location while actively in use. He disabled unnecessary tracking features and reviewed privacy settings across multiple applications. He also installed a privacy-focused browser and began paying closer attention to app permissions before granting access.

Several weeks later, Daniel noticed subtle changes. Personalized advertisements became less precise. Certain apps requested permissions that he had never questioned before, and he found himself evaluating each request more carefully. His awareness had fundamentally changed how he interacted with technology.

At work, Daniel shared some of his discoveries with colleagues. During lunch breaks, conversations frequently turned toward privacy, cybersecurity, and mobile security. Many coworkers admitted they had never considered how much information apps collected. Several began reviewing their own settings after hearing Daniel's experiences.

One coworker, Jennifer, discovered that multiple apps were tracking her location continuously despite having no obvious need for that information. Another colleague found several old apps that still retained extensive permissions even though they were rarely used. These discoveries reinforced the importance of regular privacy reviews.

Months passed, and Daniel continued refining his digital habits. He became more selective about which apps he installed. Before downloading new software, he researched the developer, reviewed privacy policies, and considered whether the app's benefits justified the data it might collect.

One afternoon, Daniel received a notification from his smartphone's privacy dashboard showing recent access to sensitive permissions. The report helped him identify an app that was requesting more information than expected. After reviewing its behavior, he decided to uninstall it entirely. The experience demonstrated the value of monitoring tools and reinforced his commitment to privacy awareness.

As his understanding grew, Daniel realized that privacy was not about avoiding technology. It was about using technology responsibly. He still enjoyed social media, navigation apps, online shopping, and streaming services. The difference was that he now understood how these systems operated and could make informed decisions about the information he shared.

Looking back, Daniel appreciated how a simple conversation over coffee had changed his perspective. What began as curiosity had evolved into a deeper understanding of the digital world. He no longer assumed that privacy protections happened automatically. Instead, he recognized that privacy required awareness, attention, and occasional action.

Most importantly, Daniel learned that even small changes could produce meaningful results. Adjusting permissions, limiting tracking, reviewing settings, and staying informed required relatively little effort. Yet these habits significantly improved his control over personal information.

His experience reflected an important truth about modern technology. Every smartphone user generates data. Every app collects information. Every digital interaction leaves a trace. While tracking may never disappear entirely, individuals have the power to reduce unnecessary exposure and make informed choices about their digital lives.

The lesson stayed with Daniel whenever he installed a new application or reviewed a permission request. Technology would continue evolving, but the principle remained constant: understanding how systems work is the first step toward protecting yourself. Through awareness, education, and proactive habits, users can navigate the digital world with greater confidence, security, and control over their personal information.

*Chapter 4*

# Reading Privacy Policies and Identifying Red Flags

One of the most overlooked aspects of mobile security and privacy protection is the privacy policy. Nearly every mobile application, website, online service, and digital platform provides a privacy policy that explains how user information is collected, stored, processed, shared, and protected. Unfortunately, most users never read these documents. Studies consistently show that the majority of people simply click "Accept" when presented with terms and privacy notices without reviewing the details. While privacy policies can sometimes be lengthy and difficult to understand, learning how to identify key sections and recognize warning signs can dramatically improve your ability to protect personal information.

Privacy policies exist for several reasons. In many countries, laws require organizations to disclose how they collect and use personal data. Privacy policies also help companies establish legal agreements with users and provide transparency regarding data practices. While some organizations genuinely prioritize transparency and user privacy, others may include broad language that allows extensive data collection and sharing. Understanding the difference is essential for making informed decisions about which applications deserve your trust.

One of the first things users should look for in a privacy policy is a clear explanation of what information is collected. Reputable companies typically provide detailed descriptions of the types of data they gather. This may include personal information such as names, email addresses, phone numbers, physical addresses, payment information, and account credentials. It may also include technical information such as device identifiers, IP addresses, operating system details, browsing activity, location data, and usage statistics.

When reviewing a privacy policy, pay close attention to whether the information being collected seems reasonable for the application's intended purpose. A banking application may legitimately require financial information and identity verification data. A navigation app may need location access. However, if a simple game or flashlight app requests extensive personal information without a clear explanation, that should raise concerns. Data collection should generally align with the app's functionality.

Another critical section involves how collected information is used. Organizations often gather data for purposes such as account management, customer support, security monitoring, service improvement, personalization, marketing, analytics, and advertising. While some uses are necessary for providing services, others may extend far beyond what users expect. Users should carefully evaluate whether they are comfortable with the stated uses of their information.

Data sharing practices deserve particularly close attention. Many privacy policies disclose that user information may be shared with third parties. These third parties can include advertisers, analytics providers, marketing partners, payment processors, cloud service providers, social media companies, and business affiliates. The more broadly information is shared, the greater the potential privacy risk. Whenever possible, users should favor applications that minimize third-party data sharing and clearly explain who receives information and why.

The term "business partners" often appears in privacy policies. While this phrase may sound harmless, it can sometimes represent a broad category of organizations that receive user information. Users should look for specific descriptions rather than vague language. Transparency is generally a positive sign. Policies that clearly identify partners and explain data-sharing practices are often more trustworthy than those relying on broad, undefined terms.

Another important consideration involves data retention policies. Data retention refers to how long organizations keep user information. Some companies retain information only as long as necessary to provide services, while others may store data indefinitely. The longer information is retained, the greater the risk of exposure through breaches, unauthorized access, or misuse. Privacy-conscious users should pay attention to retention periods and favor organizations that limit unnecessary storage.

Users should also review policies regarding user rights and controls. Modern privacy regulations increasingly require organizations to provide options for accessing, correcting, deleting, or exporting personal information. Privacy policies should explain how users can exercise these rights. Companies that make privacy controls accessible and straightforward often demonstrate stronger commitments to user privacy.

Location data deserves special attention within privacy policies. Location information is among the most sensitive categories of personal data because it can reveal daily routines, workplaces, homes, social relationships, travel patterns, and lifestyle habits. Users should carefully review how location data is collected, used, stored, and shared. Policies that permit extensive location tracking or broad sharing of location information should be evaluated cautiously.

Advertising and marketing sections often reveal how organizations monetize user information. Many free applications rely on advertising revenue. Privacy policies may describe how advertising networks collect behavioral information, track user activity, and deliver targeted advertisements. Understanding these practices helps users evaluate whether the privacy tradeoffs are acceptable.

One common red flag involves overly broad language. Statements such as "we may collect any information necessary to improve services" provide little transparency regarding actual data practices. Similarly, phrases like "we may share information with trusted partners" without identifying those partners can create uncertainty about how information is handled. Clear, specific language is generally preferable to vague descriptions.

Another warning sign is excessive data collection. If an application gathers significantly more information than appears necessary for its functionality, users should question why that information is being collected. Data minimization is a core privacy principle. Organizations that collect only necessary information generally present lower privacy risks than those gathering large volumes of unrelated data.

Poor security disclosures can also indicate potential concerns. Privacy policies should explain how information is protected through security measures such as encryption, access controls, monitoring systems, and secure storage practices. While companies are unlikely to disclose detailed security architectures, they should provide reasonable assurances regarding data protection efforts.

Changes to privacy policies represent another area users should monitor. Many organizations reserve the right to update policies over time. Users should pay attention to notifications regarding policy changes and periodically review updates. Significant changes may alter how information is collected, shared, or used. Remaining informed helps users maintain control over their privacy choices.

Children's privacy provisions are particularly important for families. Applications directed toward children should include specific protections regarding data collection, parental consent, and information sharing. Parents should carefully review privacy practices before allowing children to use applications that collect personal information.

International data transfers have become increasingly common as cloud computing and global services expand. Privacy policies may disclose that information is stored or processed in different countries. Users should understand where their data may be transferred and what legal protections apply in those jurisdictions.

One useful strategy involves comparing privacy policies across similar applications. If two apps provide comparable functionality but one collects significantly less information, the privacy-conscious choice may be obvious. Competition often encourages developers to improve privacy practices, and users can support these efforts by favoring organizations that prioritize data protection.

Privacy policies should not be viewed as mere legal formalities. They are valuable tools that provide insight into how organizations treat user information. While reading every word may not always be practical, understanding how to identify key sections and recognize red flags empowers users to make better decisions.

Ultimately, privacy protection begins with informed consent. Consent is only meaningful when users understand what they are agreeing to. By learning how to evaluate privacy policies critically, users gain greater visibility into data practices and reduce the likelihood of unpleasant surprises. Knowledge, awareness, and careful evaluation remain among the strongest defenses against unnecessary data collection and privacy risks in the digital age.

### *Rachel attended a technology conference*

Rachel loved discovering new mobile apps. Whether it was productivity tools, fitness trackers, budgeting software, or entertainment platforms, she was always searching for ways to make life more efficient. Like most people, however, she rarely paid attention to privacy policies.

Whenever she downloaded a new application, she would scroll quickly to the bottom of the agreement and tap "Accept." The lengthy legal documents seemed impossible to understand and felt like little more than formalities standing between her and the app she wanted to use.

One day, Rachel attended a technology conference organized by her employer. During a cybersecurity presentation, the speaker discussed privacy policies and explained how they often reveal more about an application's true intentions than its marketing materials.

The presenter displayed excerpts from several privacy policies. One application collected extensive location data, browsing activity, and contact information despite offering only basic weather forecasts. Another shared user information with dozens of advertising partners. The examples surprised Rachel. She had never considered how much information privacy policies could reveal.

Inspired by the presentation, Rachel decided to examine the apps installed on her smartphone. She selected a few of her most frequently used applications and began reading their privacy policies. At first, the process felt tedious. The documents were long and filled with unfamiliar terminology. However, as she learned what to look for, patterns began to emerge.

One social media app disclosed that it collected location information, device identifiers, browsing activity, and interaction data. Another shopping app described extensive partnerships with advertising networks. A free game included broad language allowing information sharing with numerous third parties. Rachel realized that many apps were collecting far more information than she had ever imagined.

Rather than becoming alarmed, she approached the process analytically. She created a simple checklist to evaluate applications. What information was collected? Why was it needed? Was data shared with third parties? How long was information retained? Could users delete their data? The checklist helped transform privacy policy reviews from overwhelming legal exercises into manageable evaluations.

A few weeks later, Rachel encountered an app that promised advanced photo editing features. Before downloading it, she reviewed its privacy policy. The application requested access to contacts, location data, and extensive behavioral information despite focusing primarily on image editing. Several sections used vague language regarding data sharing. Based on what she had learned, Rachel decided not to install the app.

Instead, she researched alternative photo editors and found another application with a much more transparent privacy policy. The second app collected significantly less information and clearly explained its practices. The experience demonstrated how privacy awareness could influence decision-making before risks emerged.

As Rachel continued developing her privacy skills, she shared her experiences with friends and family. During a weekend gathering, she showed her younger brother how to identify key sections within privacy policies. He was surprised to discover that one of his favorite apps retained user information indefinitely and shared data with numerous partners.

The conversation sparked interest among several family members. Soon, they were comparing privacy practices across different applications and discussing which companies appeared more trustworthy. What began as a personal learning experience evolved into a shared effort to improve digital awareness.

Months later, Rachel noticed a significant change in her relationship with technology. She still enjoyed using apps and digital services, but she approached them with greater understanding. Rather than assuming all applications operated similarly, she recognized that developers made different choices regarding privacy and data collection.

One evening, Rachel received an email announcing updates to the privacy policy of a service she used regularly. In the past, she would have ignored the notification. This time, she reviewed the changes carefully. The update expanded certain data-sharing practices. After considering the implications, she adjusted her account settings to limit optional data collection.

That small decision reinforced an important lesson. Privacy protection was not a one-time task. It required ongoing awareness and occasional adjustments as technologies and policies evolved.

Over the following years, Rachel became known among friends as someone who understood digital privacy. People frequently asked her questions about apps, permissions, tracking, and security settings. While she never considered herself a cybersecurity expert, she appreciated how much she had learned simply by paying attention to information that most users ignored.

Looking back, Rachel realized that privacy policies were not designed solely for lawyers and regulators. They were tools that empowered users to understand how organizations handled personal information. While the documents were not always easy to read, they contained valuable insights for anyone willing to look.

The experience changed her perspective on technology. Convenience remained important, but so did transparency and trust. Applications that respected user privacy earned her confidence. Those that relied on excessive collection or vague disclosures did not.

Most importantly, Rachel learned that informed decisions create stronger privacy outcomes. Every app installation, account creation, and permission request represented a choice. By understanding privacy policies, she gained the information needed to make those choices wisely.

Her journey illustrated a simple but powerful truth: users cannot control every aspect of the digital world, but they can control which organizations receive their trust. Privacy policies provide one of the clearest windows into how that trust will be handled. Learning to read them effectively is a skill that benefits every smartphone user, regardless of age, profession, or technical background.

As technology continued advancing, Rachel knew new privacy challenges would emerge. Yet she also understood that the principles she had learned—awareness, evaluation, and informed decision-making—would remain valuable. Armed with those principles, she felt prepared to navigate the digital future with greater confidence, security, and control over her personal information.

## Chapter 5

# Securing App Accounts, Passwords, and Authentication

One of the most important aspects of mobile app security involves protecting the accounts that connect users to their applications. Whether accessing banking apps, social media platforms, email services, cloud storage accounts, messaging applications, shopping platforms, healthcare portals, or productivity tools, users rely on account credentials to prove their identity and gain access to personal information. Unfortunately, cybercriminals understand the value of these accounts and continuously develop new methods to steal credentials, bypass security measures, and gain unauthorized access. Learning how to secure app accounts is one of the most effective ways to protect your privacy, finances, identity, and digital life.

Every account begins with authentication. Authentication is the process of verifying that a user is who they claim to be. Traditionally, authentication relied primarily on passwords. A user would create a username and password combination, and the system would grant access if the credentials matched stored records. While passwords remain a critical component of account security, modern cybersecurity experts recognize that passwords alone are often insufficient against today's threats.

One of the biggest problems with passwords is that many users choose weak or predictable combinations. Common passwords such as "123456," "password," birthdays, pet names, and simple dictionary words remain surprisingly widespread. Cybercriminals use automated tools capable of testing millions of common passwords within minutes. Weak passwords significantly increase the likelihood of unauthorized access and should be avoided entirely.

A strong password should be long, unique, and difficult to guess. Modern security recommendations emphasize length over complexity alone. A password containing sixteen or more characters generally provides greater protection than a shorter password filled with symbols. Combining uppercase letters, lowercase letters, numbers, and special characters further strengthens security. However, the most important factor is uniqueness. Every account should have its own password.

Password reuse represents one of the most dangerous habits in digital security. Many people use the same password across multiple accounts because it is easier to remember. Unfortunately, if one account becomes compromised through a data breach, cybercriminals often attempt to use the stolen credentials on other platforms. This technique, known as credential stuffing, allows attackers to gain access to multiple accounts using a single leaked password. Unique passwords prevent one compromised account from creating a chain reaction across a user's digital life.

Password managers provide an effective solution to the challenge of managing numerous unique passwords. A password manager is a secure application that stores, generates, and organizes passwords. Instead of memorizing dozens or hundreds of credentials, users only need to remember one strong master password. Password managers can automatically generate highly secure passwords and fill them into applications when needed. This encourages stronger security practices while improving convenience.

Multi-factor authentication, commonly called MFA, represents one of the most important advancements in account security. MFA requires users to provide two or more forms of verification before gaining access. Typically, this involves something the user knows, such as a password, combined with something the user possesses, such as a smartphone or authentication device. Even if an attacker steals a password, they may still be unable to access the account without the second authentication factor.

Several forms of multi-factor authentication exist. One common method involves receiving a temporary verification code via text message. Another uses authentication apps that generate time-based codes. Hardware security keys provide even stronger protection by requiring physical possession of a dedicated device. Biometric authentication methods such as fingerprints and facial recognition can also serve as additional verification factors. Whenever possible, users should enable MFA on important accounts.

Authentication applications often provide stronger protection than text-message verification. While SMS-based authentication is better than relying solely on passwords, text messages can sometimes be intercepted through techniques such as SIM-swapping attacks. Authentication apps generate codes directly on the user's device, reducing exposure to certain forms of attack. Many cybersecurity professionals recommend using authentication apps whenever available.

Biometric authentication has become increasingly common on mobile devices. Fingerprint scanners and facial recognition systems allow users to unlock devices and access applications quickly. These technologies offer convenience while adding an additional layer of security. However, users should understand that biometric authentication is not infallible. It should complement strong passwords and other security measures rather than replace them entirely.

Cybercriminals frequently use phishing attacks to steal account credentials. Phishing involves creating fraudulent messages, emails, websites, or notifications designed to trick users into revealing sensitive information. A phishing message may appear to come from a trusted company and encourage users to log in through a fake website. Once credentials are entered, attackers capture the information and use it to access legitimate accounts. Learning to recognize phishing attempts is essential for account security.

Signs of phishing often include urgent language, unexpected requests for personal information, suspicious links, spelling errors, unusual sender addresses, and threats regarding account suspension. Users should avoid clicking links in unsolicited messages and instead navigate directly to official websites or applications when verifying account information.

Account recovery options deserve careful attention as well. Many services provide recovery methods that allow users to regain access if credentials are forgotten. Recovery options may include backup email addresses, phone numbers, security questions, recovery codes, or trusted devices. While these features improve accessibility, they can also create vulnerabilities if not secured properly. Users should regularly review recovery settings and ensure they remain accurate and protected.

Security questions were once widely used for account recovery. Unfortunately, many security questions rely on information that can be discovered through social media, public records, or personal conversations. Questions about pets, schools, birthdays, or family members may not provide meaningful security. Whenever possible, users should choose more secure recovery methods.

Regular monitoring of account activity provides another important layer of protection. Many applications offer account activity logs showing login attempts, device access history, and security events. Reviewing these logs periodically can help users identify suspicious behavior before serious damage occurs. Unexpected logins, unfamiliar devices, or unusual account activity should be investigated immediately.

Notifications and alerts can significantly enhance account security. Many platforms allow users to receive notifications when passwords are changed, new devices are added, unusual login attempts occur, or sensitive account settings are modified. Enabling these alerts increases visibility and provides early warning of potential threats.

Public Wi-Fi networks introduce additional authentication risks. Cybercriminals sometimes attempt to intercept communications or create fraudulent networks designed to capture credentials. Users should exercise caution when logging into sensitive accounts on public networks. Whenever possible, secure connections and virtual private networks should be used when accessing important services.

Software updates also contribute to authentication security. Mobile operating systems and applications regularly release updates that address vulnerabilities, improve encryption, and strengthen security mechanisms. Delaying updates can leave users exposed to known weaknesses that attackers may exploit. Keeping devices and applications current is an essential security practice.

Organizations increasingly implement advanced authentication technologies such as risk-based authentication and behavioral analysis. These systems evaluate factors such as device characteristics, login locations, typing patterns, and usage behavior to identify suspicious activity. While users may not always notice these protections, they contribute significantly to modern account security.

Ultimately, securing app accounts requires a layered approach. Strong passwords, unique credentials, password managers, multi-factor authentication, phishing awareness, recovery security, monitoring tools, and regular updates all contribute to a comprehensive defense strategy. No single measure provides complete protection, but together they create multiple barriers that make unauthorized access far more difficult.

The digital world continues expanding, and the number of accounts most people manage grows every year. Banking services, healthcare systems, social media platforms, cloud storage providers, educational portals, shopping websites, and workplace applications all rely on authentication systems. By mastering account security fundamentals, users gain one of the most powerful tools available for protecting personal information and maintaining control over their digital identities.

### *He knew cybersecurity experts recommended unique passwords*

Kevin considered himself a careful person. He paid bills on time, locked his doors at night, and kept important documents organized. Yet when it came to digital security, he had developed habits that would eventually create serious problems.

Like many people, Kevin used the same password for nearly everything. His email account, social media profiles, shopping websites, streaming services, and several financial applications all shared variations of the same password. He knew cybersecurity experts recommended unique passwords, but managing dozens of credentials seemed inconvenient.

For years, nothing happened. His accounts functioned normally, and he saw no reason to change his habits.

One afternoon, Kevin received an email from an online retailer where he occasionally purchased electronics. The company announced that it had experienced a data breach and advised customers to change their passwords. Kevin read the notification but assumed the risk was minimal. After all, the retailer only stored limited information.

A few weeks later, strange things began occurring. He received notifications about login attempts on his email account. Shortly afterward, his social media profile displayed posts he had not created. Then his streaming service reported that someone had logged in from another country.

At first, Kevin thought the incidents were unrelated. However, when he attempted to access one of his accounts and discovered the password had been changed, he realized something was wrong.

Concerned, he contacted customer support and began investigating. Through conversations with security representatives, Kevin learned about credential stuffing attacks. Attackers had likely obtained his password from the retailer's data breach and then tested the same credentials across multiple services. Because he reused passwords, the attack succeeded.

The experience was frustrating and stressful. Recovering accounts required identity verification, password resets, and hours of communication with support teams. Some accounts were easier to recover than others. The process exposed just how interconnected his digital life had become.

Determined not to repeat the mistake, Kevin began learning about account security. He researched password managers, multi-factor authentication, phishing attacks, and authentication applications. The more he learned, the more he realized how vulnerable his previous approach had been.

His first step was installing a reputable password manager. The software generated long, unique passwords for every account. Initially, the change felt overwhelming. He had dozens of accounts to update. However, once the process was complete, managing passwords became surprisingly easy.

Next, Kevin enabled multi-factor authentication on all critical accounts. Email services, banking applications, cloud storage platforms, and social media accounts now required an additional verification code during login. Although the extra step added a few seconds to the process, the increased security provided peace of mind.

Several months later, Kevin received another security alert. An attacker had attempted to access one of his accounts using an old password from a previous breach. This time, however, the attempt failed. The password was no longer valid, and the attacker could not provide the required authentication code.

The notification reinforced the value of the changes Kevin had made. His security measures were working exactly as intended.

Around the same time, Kevin's friend Melissa encountered a phishing attack. She received a message claiming her bank account required immediate verification. The email appeared legitimate and included official logos and branding. Fortunately, before entering her credentials, she asked Kevin for advice.

After reviewing the message, Kevin identified several warning signs. The sender address was unusual, the message contained subtle spelling errors, and the provided link led to a suspicious website. Melissa avoided becoming a victim because she recognized the red flags.

Their conversation highlighted another important lesson: technology alone cannot solve every security problem. Awareness and education remain essential components of protection.

As years passed, Kevin continued refining his security practices. He reviewed account activity regularly, updated passwords when necessary, monitored security alerts, and stayed informed about emerging threats. What once seemed complicated had become routine.

Most importantly, he no longer viewed cybersecurity as an inconvenience. Instead, he recognized it as a practical investment in protecting his finances, privacy, reputation, and personal information.

Looking back, Kevin realized that the data breach had provided a valuable wake-up call. While the experience had been stressful, it motivated him to adopt habits that significantly improved his security. The lessons he learned transformed the way he approached digital life.

Today, whenever someone asks for cybersecurity advice, Kevin shares the same message: start with your accounts. Strong passwords, unique credentials, password managers, and multi-factor authentication provide extraordinary protection relative to the effort required. Small actions taken today can prevent major problems tomorrow.

His experience demonstrated a truth that cybersecurity professionals emphasize repeatedly. Attackers often seek the easiest targets. By implementing multiple layers of protection, users dramatically reduce their risk and make unauthorized access far more difficult.

For Kevin, account security was no longer an abstract concept discussed only by experts. It had become a personal responsibility and an essential part of modern life. Through knowledge, preparation, and consistent habits, he had transformed a painful lesson into lasting protection.

The digital world would continue evolving, and new threats would certainly emerge. Yet Kevin felt confident knowing he possessed the tools and knowledge necessary to adapt. By securing his accounts and understanding authentication principles, he had taken one of the most important steps toward protecting his digital future.

## Chapter [illegible]

# Identifying Malicious Apps & Mobile Scams

As smartphones have become essential tools for communication, banking, shopping, entertainment, and productivity, cybercriminals have increasingly shifted their attention toward mobile devices. While app stores provide millions of genuine applications that improve daily life, they also attract criminals seeking to exploit unsuspecting users. Malicious apps, fake apps, fraudulent software, and mobile scams have become one of the fastest-growing threats, capable of compromising privacy, stealing financial information, hijacking accounts, and infecting devices with malware. Understanding how these threats operate is one of the most critical skills every smartphone user can develop.

A malicious app is any application intentionally designed to harm users, steal information, generate unauthorized profits, or provide unauthorized access to a device. Unlike legitimate applications that offer genuine functionality, malicious apps often disguise their true purpose behind attractive features, deceptive marketing, or counterfeit branding. Once installed, these apps may collect personal information, display excessive advertisements, monitor user activity, steal passwords, record

*Chapter 6*

# Identifying Malicious Apps, Fake Apps, and Mobile Scams

As smartphones have become essential tools for communication, banking, shopping, entertainment, and productivity, cybercriminals have increasingly shifted their attention toward mobile devices. While app stores provide millions of legitimate applications that improve daily life, they also attract criminals seeking to exploit unsuspecting users. Malicious apps, fake apps, fraudulent software, and mobile scams have become major cybersecurity threats capable of compromising privacy, stealing financial information, hijacking accounts, and infecting devices with malware. Understanding how these threats operate is one of the most important skills every smartphone user can develop.

A malicious app is any application intentionally designed to harm users, steal information, generate unauthorized profits, or provide unauthorized access to a device. Unlike legitimate applications that offer genuine functionality, malicious apps often disguise their true purpose behind attractive features, deceptive marketing, or counterfeit branding. Once installed, these apps may collect personal information, display excessive advertisements, monitor user activity, steal passwords, record keystrokes, access financial accounts, or download additional malware.

One of the most common forms of mobile threats involves fake applications. Fake apps are designed to imitate legitimate software in order to trick users into downloading them. Cybercriminals often copy the names, logos, screenshots, and descriptions of popular apps to create convincing counterfeits. At first glance, these fake versions may appear nearly identical to genuine applications. However, once installed, they may steal login credentials, collect personal information, or compromise device security.

Fake banking applications are particularly dangerous. Cybercriminals know that financial information is highly valuable, so they frequently create counterfeit banking apps that resemble legitimate institutions. Users who enter usernames, passwords, account numbers, or authentication codes into these fake applications may unknowingly provide direct access to their financial accounts. Verifying the authenticity of financial applications before installation is therefore essential.

Social media platforms are also common targets for impersonation. Fake versions of popular messaging and social networking apps may promise enhanced features, premium access, or exclusive capabilities. In reality, these apps often exist solely to harvest credentials or install malicious software. Users should always download applications from trusted sources and verify the developer's identity before installation.

Another major threat category involves spyware. Spyware is malicious software designed to monitor user activity without consent. Mobile spyware can collect messages, emails, browsing history, location data, call logs, photos, contacts, and other sensitive information. Some advanced spyware applications operate quietly in the background, making detection difficult. The information gathered may be sold, used for identity theft, or exploited for blackmail and fraud.

Adware represents another widespread mobile threat. While not always as dangerous as spyware, adware generates excessive advertisements that disrupt device functionality and create privacy concerns. Some adware applications collect extensive behavioral data to support advertising operations. Others display misleading notifications designed to trick users into downloading additional software or visiting fraudulent websites.

Trojans are among the most dangerous forms of mobile malware. A Trojan disguises itself as a legitimate application while secretly performing malicious actions. Once installed, a

Trojan may steal credentials, monitor activity, create backdoors for attackers, or download additional malicious programs. Because Trojans often appear useful or desirable, they rely heavily on social engineering rather than technical vulnerabilities.

Ransomware, although more commonly associated with computers, has also affected mobile devices. Mobile ransomware may lock users out of their devices, encrypt files, or display intimidating messages demanding payment. While mobile ransomware is less common than other forms of malware, its potential impact can be severe. Regular backups and strong security practices help reduce ransomware risks.

One important warning sign involves excessive permission requests. Legitimate applications generally request permissions that support their intended functionality. If a simple flashlight app requests access to contacts, location services, microphones, and messaging functions, users should question why such access is necessary. Excessive permissions often indicate unnecessary data collection or malicious intent.

Poor reviews and suspicious ratings can also provide valuable clues. Before installing an application, users should review ratings, comments, and feedback from other users. Consistent complaints about privacy concerns, excessive advertising, unexpected behavior, or fraudulent activity should be taken seriously. While fake reviews do exist, patterns often emerge that help identify problematic applications.

Developer reputation is another critical factor when evaluating app safety. Legitimate developers typically maintain professional websites, provide contact information, publish privacy policies, and establish a history of trustworthy software. Unknown developers with little transparency or limited track records should be approached cautiously. Verifying the developer's identity helps reduce the likelihood of installing malicious software.

Users should also pay attention to download numbers. Popular legitimate applications often have millions of downloads and substantial user communities. While new applications are not automatically suspicious, apps claiming to replicate major services yet possessing very few downloads may warrant closer scrutiny.

Scareware represents another common mobile threat. Scareware applications display alarming messages claiming that a device is infected, compromised, or operating improperly. These warnings are designed to create panic and pressure users into purchasing unnecessary services or installing additional software. Legitimate operating systems rarely display security warnings through random advertisements or pop-up messages.

Phishing applications and phishing websites frequently work together. A malicious app may direct users to counterfeit login pages that closely resemble legitimate websites. Once credentials are entered, attackers capture the information and use it to access real accounts. Users should carefully verify URLs, application authenticity, and login screens before entering sensitive information.

Cybercriminals also exploit current events, trends, and emergencies. During major news events, natural disasters, public health crises, or popular product launches, attackers often release fake apps designed to capitalize on public interest. Users should be especially cautious when downloading applications related to breaking news or rapidly developing situations.

Official app stores provide important security benefits but do not eliminate all risks. Google Play and Apple's App Store review applications before publication and remove many malicious programs. However, some malicious apps occasionally bypass screening processes. Therefore, users should continue evaluating apps carefully even when downloading from trusted marketplaces.

Keeping operating systems and applications updated significantly improves security. Updates frequently contain patches that address vulnerabilities, improve malware detection capabilities, and strengthen overall device protection. Delaying updates can leave users exposed to known threats that attackers actively target.

Mobile security software can provide additional protection by scanning applications, monitoring behavior, detecting malware, and warning users about potential threats. While no security solution is perfect, reputable mobile security tools can serve as valuable layers of defense.

Education remains one of the most effective protections against malicious apps and scams. Cybercriminals frequently rely on deception rather than technical sophistication. Users who understand common attack techniques are far less likely to become victims. Developing healthy skepticism, verifying sources, reviewing permissions, and researching applications before installation dramatically reduces risk.

Ultimately, identifying malicious apps requires a combination of awareness, caution, and informed decision-making. No single warning sign guarantees that an app is dangerous, but patterns of suspicious behavior often reveal underlying risks. By learning to recognize these warning signs and adopting proactive security habits, users can significantly improve their ability to avoid scams, protect personal information, and maintain control over their mobile devices.

***Tyler assumed the problems were unrelated***

Tyler enjoyed experimenting with new technology. As a freelance graphic designer, he relied heavily on mobile apps for productivity, communication, file management, and creative projects. He frequently searched for tools that could improve efficiency or provide new features.

One evening, while browsing online forums, Tyler discovered discussions about a new photo editing app that promised advanced artificial intelligence features. Users claimed the app could enhance images automatically and produce professional-quality results with minimal effort. Excited by the possibilities, Tyler searched for the application.

Several versions appeared in the app store. One had thousands of downloads and professional branding. Another appeared nearly identical but offered additional premium features for free. The second version caught Tyler's attention because it seemed more generous than the official release.

Without conducting much research, he downloaded the alternative version.

Initially, everything seemed normal. The app launched successfully and provided basic editing functionality. However, within a few days, Tyler noticed unusual behavior. Advertisements appeared constantly, even when the app was not open. Battery life decreased significantly. The phone occasionally became sluggish and unresponsive.

At first, Tyler assumed the problems were unrelated. He blamed software updates, heavy usage, and aging hardware. However, the issues continued worsening. Strange notifications appeared regularly, and his browser occasionally redirected to unfamiliar websites.

Concerned, Tyler began investigating. He reviewed the app's permissions and was surprised to discover extensive access rights. The photo editor possessed location permissions, contact access, storage permissions, and several other capabilities unrelated to image editing. The realization immediately raised concerns.

After conducting additional research, Tyler discovered online reports identifying the application as a fraudulent clone of the legitimate software. Cybersecurity researchers had linked the app to aggressive advertising networks and data collection practices. The app was not the official version at all.

Tyler immediately removed the application and ran a security scan using a reputable mobile security tool. The scan identified several suspicious components associated with the fake app. Fortunately, no major damage appeared to have occurred, but the experience served as an important lesson.

Determined to avoid similar mistakes, Tyler began studying mobile security practices. He learned how fake apps impersonated legitimate software, how cybercriminals manipulated app store listings, and how excessive permissions often indicated underlying problems. The more he learned, the more he realized how easily users could be deceived.

Several months later, Tyler encountered another suspicious app while searching for a budgeting tool. This time, he approached the evaluation differently. He reviewed the developer's information, examined user reviews, checked download statistics, researched the company online, and analyzed the permissions being requested.

The investigation revealed several red flags. Reviews mentioned unusual advertisements and privacy concerns. The developer had no professional website. The permissions appeared excessive for a budgeting application. Based on these findings, Tyler decided not to install the software.

His decision was later validated when the app was removed from the marketplace following reports of malicious behavior.

Around the same time, Tyler's friend Samantha experienced a mobile scam. She received a pop-up message claiming her smartphone was infected with dangerous malware. The warning instructed her to install a recommended security application immediately.

Panicked, Samantha nearly followed the instructions. Fortunately, she contacted Tyler before taking action.

After reviewing the warning, Tyler recognized it as scareware. The message was designed to create fear and pressure users into installing potentially harmful software. He explained how legitimate operating systems rarely display security warnings through random advertisements and encouraged Samantha to close the browser instead.

Relieved, Samantha avoided becoming another victim.

These experiences reinforced Tyler's growing understanding of cybersecurity. He realized that many threats relied less on advanced hacking techniques and more on manipulation. Attackers exploited trust, curiosity, urgency, and convenience to achieve their objectives.

As years passed, Tyler developed a structured process for evaluating applications. Before installing any software, he verified the developer's identity, reviewed permissions, examined ratings, researched online feedback, and considered whether the requested access made sense. These habits required only a few minutes but significantly reduced risk.

His smartphone experience improved as well. Fewer unnecessary apps meant fewer advertisements, better performance, improved battery life, and enhanced privacy. The benefits extended beyond security alone.

Eventually, friends and colleagues began asking Tyler for recommendations regarding mobile apps and privacy practices. He frequently shared the same advice: slow down before installing anything. A few minutes of research could prevent weeks or months of frustration.

Looking back, Tyler appreciated how a single mistake had changed his perspective. Downloading the fake photo editor had been inconvenient, but it motivated him to develop habits that strengthened his long-term security. The experience taught him that cybersecurity was not solely about technology. It was also about judgment, awareness, and informed decision-making.

The lesson remained relevant every time he opened an app store. Attractive marketing, impressive promises, and persuasive descriptions no longer guaranteed trust. Instead, Tyler looked beyond appearances and focused on evidence.

In a digital world filled with legitimate innovation as well as malicious deception, that mindset became one of his most valuable defenses. Through education, caution, and consistent habits, he transformed from an easy target into a knowledgeable user capable of navigating mobile technology safely and confidently.

His story demonstrates an essential truth about modern cybersecurity: the most effective protection often begins long before malware reaches a device. It begins with the choices users make before they click "Install." By learning to recognize warning signs and verify authenticity, individuals can avoid many threats entirely and enjoy the benefits of technology without falling victim to deception.

*Chapter 7*

# Managing App Privacy Settings for Maximum Protection

Installing a secure application is only the first step toward protecting your privacy. Many users assume that once an app is downloaded from a trusted source, their personal information is automatically protected. In reality, most mobile applications include a wide range of privacy settings that determine how information is collected, shared, stored, and used. These settings often remain configured with default options that prioritize convenience, personalization, advertising, or data collection rather than privacy. Learning how to manage app privacy settings effectively is one of the most powerful ways to take control of your digital footprint and strengthen your overall mobile security.

Every application is designed with a balance between functionality and data collection. Developers often gather information to improve services, personalize content, deliver advertisements, analyze user behavior, and generate revenue. While some of these activities are legitimate and beneficial, users should understand that default settings are not always optimized for privacy. Taking a few minutes to review and adjust privacy settings can significantly reduce unnecessary data exposure.

The first step in managing privacy settings is understanding what information an application collects. Most apps gather at least some combination of personal information, device information, usage statistics, location data, and behavioral analytics. Privacy settings often provide options that allow users to limit certain forms of collection without affecting the core functionality of the application. Reviewing these options should become a routine part of installing any new app.

Location privacy settings deserve special attention because location data is among the most sensitive categories of personal information. Many apps request location access even when it is not essential to their primary function. Modern operating systems provide options such as "Allow Once," "Allow While Using the App," and "Don't Allow." In most situations, limiting access to only while actively using the app provides an excellent balance between functionality and privacy. Continuous background location tracking should generally be reserved for applications that genuinely require it, such as navigation services.

Advertising preferences represent another critical privacy area. Many applications use advertising identifiers and behavioral tracking systems to build user profiles and deliver targeted advertisements. Privacy settings frequently include options to limit personalized advertising, reset advertising identifiers, or disable certain forms of tracking. While these changes may not eliminate all advertising, they can reduce the amount of behavioral information available to advertisers and data brokers.

Social media applications often contain extensive privacy controls that many users never explore. These settings may govern who can view posts, access profile information, send messages, locate users through searches, tag photos, view activity status, and interact with shared content. Carefully reviewing these options allows users to control how much information is visible to strangers, acquaintances, advertisers, and even platform operators.

Many messaging applications also include important privacy features. Users can often control who may contact them, view profile photos, see online status indicators, access read receipts, and participate in group conversations. Some messaging platforms provide end-to-end encryption settings, disappearing messages, screen lock features, and device verification tools that significantly improve communication security.

Cloud storage applications introduce another category of privacy considerations. These services often synchronize files, photos, documents, and backups across multiple devices. Privacy settings may determine who can access shared files, how links are distributed, whether metadata is collected, and how long deleted content remains recoverable. Understanding these controls helps users manage both convenience and confidentiality.

Photo-sharing applications frequently contain privacy settings related to image visibility, facial recognition, metadata collection, and location tagging. Many users do not realize that photos often contain embedded information about where and when images were captured. Privacy-conscious users should review settings related to metadata sharing and location tagging before uploading personal photos.

Health and fitness applications collect particularly sensitive information. These apps may gather exercise routines, heart rate data, sleep patterns, dietary habits, medical information, and location histories. Privacy settings often allow users to control data sharing with third parties, advertising networks, healthcare providers, and research organizations. Given the sensitivity of health information, users should carefully evaluate these options.

One often-overlooked area involves app synchronization and background activity. Many applications continue communicating with servers even when not actively being used. Privacy settings may provide controls that limit background activity, reduce data sharing, and decrease unnecessary communications. Restricting background operations can improve privacy while also conserving battery life and reducing data usage.

Contact synchronization settings deserve careful review as well. Many applications request access to address books and contact lists. While this may improve convenience by helping users connect with friends and family, it also involves sharing information about other individuals who may not have consented. Users should consider whether contact synchronization is truly necessary before enabling these features.

Email applications and productivity tools often include privacy settings related to analytics, usage reporting, smart features, and artificial intelligence integrations. While these capabilities may enhance functionality, they can also involve additional data collection. Users should understand the tradeoffs involved and configure settings according to their personal privacy preferences.

Biometric privacy settings have become increasingly important as fingerprint scanners and facial recognition technologies become more common. Many applications now support biometric authentication. While these features enhance convenience and security, users should understand how biometric information is stored, protected, and used. Reputable platforms typically store biometric data securely on the device rather than transmitting it to external servers.

Data-sharing preferences are among the most important settings users can review. Many applications provide options to participate in analytics programs, personalized advertising systems, product improvement initiatives, and third-party partnerships. While participation is often enabled by default, users can frequently opt out of certain forms of data sharing without losing access to essential services.

Privacy dashboards provided by modern operating systems offer valuable insights into app behavior. These dashboards allow users to monitor permission usage, review data access patterns, identify tracking activity, and understand how applications interact with sensitive information. Regularly reviewing these dashboards can help identify unexpected behaviors and reinforce informed decision-making.

Another important practice involves reviewing privacy settings after application updates. Developers periodically introduce new features, modify policies, and add data collection capabilities. Settings that were once configured appropriately may require adjustments following major updates. Staying informed about changes helps maintain control over personal information over time.

Children and family devices require special privacy considerations. Parents should review app settings carefully before allowing children to use applications that collect personal information. Privacy protections should be tailored to the child's age, maturity level, and online activities. Family-focused privacy settings often provide valuable tools for protecting younger users.

The concept of privacy by default has gained significant attention within the cybersecurity community. Ideally, applications should launch with the most privacy-protective settings enabled automatically. Unfortunately, many apps still prioritize data collection over privacy. Until privacy-by-default becomes universal, users must take responsibility for reviewing and adjusting settings themselves.

Managing privacy settings is not a one-time task. Technology evolves, applications change, and new features emerge regularly. Privacy protection requires ongoing attention and periodic reviews. Fortunately, most adjustments take only a few minutes and can produce substantial benefits.

Ultimately, privacy settings represent opportunities for users to customize how technology interacts with their personal information. Every setting reflects a choice regarding visibility, accessibility, sharing, and control. By understanding these options and making deliberate decisions, users can enjoy the benefits of modern applications while minimizing unnecessary exposure. The goal is not to eliminate functionality but to ensure that technology operates according to the user's preferences rather than the developer's default assumptions.

### *She considered herself relatively knowledgeable about technology*

Sophia loved technology. As a marketing consultant, she used dozens of mobile applications every day to communicate with clients, manage projects, schedule appointments, create content, and stay informed about industry trends. Her smartphone served as a portable office that traveled with her everywhere.

Despite her professional reliance on technology, Sophia rarely paid attention to privacy settings. She downloaded applications, accepted default configurations, and focused on getting work done. As long as the apps functioned properly, she assumed everything was fine.

One afternoon, Sophia attended a cybersecurity seminar hosted by a local business association. During the presentation, a privacy expert demonstrated how much information popular apps collected under default settings. The speaker showed examples of social media platforms sharing activity data, fitness apps tracking location histories, and shopping applications collecting behavioral information.

Sophia was surprised. She considered herself relatively knowledgeable about technology, yet she had never examined most of the privacy settings on her own device.

That evening, curiosity led her to explore her smartphone's privacy dashboard. The information was eye-opening. Several applications had accessed her location repeatedly throughout the day. Others maintained extensive permissions that she had forgotten granting months earlier. Some apps participated in personalized advertising programs she had never knowingly enabled.

Rather than feeling alarmed, Sophia became determined to understand her options.

She started with social media platforms. As she explored the settings menus, she discovered numerous controls related to profile visibility, searchability, activity status, advertising preferences, and data sharing. Many features were configured to maximize visibility and engagement rather than privacy.

Over the next several days, Sophia systematically reviewed each category. She limited who could view personal information, disabled unnecessary data sharing, restricted advertising personalization, and adjusted profile visibility settings. The process took time, but she appreciated learning how much control was available.

Next, she examined location settings. Several applications possessed continuous access to location services despite having no obvious need for background tracking. She changed most permissions to "While Using the App" and removed location access entirely from apps that did not require it.

The changes had little impact on functionality. Navigation apps continued working. Weather services still provided forecasts. Yet her device no longer shared location information continuously with multiple applications.

Encouraged by the results, Sophia reviewed messaging platforms, cloud storage services, fitness applications, and productivity tools. Each app contained settings she had never previously considered. Some allowed data sharing with partners. Others offered analytics opt-outs. Many provided options to reduce information collection without sacrificing key features.

Several weeks later, Sophia noticed a subtle but meaningful shift in her perspective. She no longer viewed privacy as something controlled entirely by technology companies. Instead, she recognized that users often possessed significant influence over how information was handled.

One day, her colleague Marcus mentioned concerns about targeted advertisements appearing after discussing specific products. The conversation reminded Sophia of her recent discoveries. She explained how privacy settings, advertising preferences, and tracking controls influenced the information available to advertisers.

Marcus admitted he had never reviewed his privacy settings. Intrigued, he began exploring his own device. A few days later, he thanked Sophia for encouraging him to investigate. He had identified several settings he wanted to adjust and felt more informed about his digital footprint.

The experience reinforced an important lesson. Many privacy improvements did not require advanced technical expertise.

Instead, they required awareness and a willingness to explore available options.

Months later, Sophia made privacy reviews part of her routine. Whenever she installed a new application, she examined permissions and privacy settings before fully integrating the app into her workflow. She also reviewed existing apps periodically to ensure configurations remained aligned with her preferences.

One particularly useful habit involved checking settings after major updates. On several occasions, she discovered new features and revised privacy options introduced by developers. Staying informed helped her maintain control over evolving technologies.

As her understanding grew, Sophia began viewing privacy settings as personal boundaries. Just as she controlled who entered her home, accessed her office, or viewed sensitive documents, she could also influence how digital services interacted with her information. Privacy was not about secrecy. It was about choice.

Looking back, Sophia realized how much control she had surrendered simply by accepting default configurations. Developers designed those defaults for broad audiences and business objectives. They did not necessarily reflect her individual priorities.

By taking time to review and adjust settings, she aligned technology with her own preferences rather than relying on assumptions made by others.

The lesson extended beyond smartphones. Sophia began evaluating privacy options across websites, online services, smart devices, and digital platforms. The same principles applied everywhere: understand what information is collected, determine how it is used, and make deliberate choices about sharing.

Her journey demonstrated that privacy protection often involves a series of small decisions rather than dramatic actions. Each adjusted setting reduced unnecessary exposure and increased personal control. Individually, the changes seemed minor. Collectively, they created a meaningful improvement in privacy and security.

As technology continued evolving, Sophia knew new privacy challenges would emerge. Yet she felt confident because she had developed a mindset centered on awareness, evaluation, and intentional decision-making.

The smartphone in her pocket remained as useful as ever. The difference was that it now operated more closely according to her preferences rather than the default expectations of countless developers and advertisers.

That realization became one of the most valuable lessons of her digital life. Privacy settings were not hidden technical details meant only for experts. They were practical tools that empowered ordinary users to shape their own digital experiences. By learning how to use those tools effectively, anyone could take meaningful steps toward greater privacy, security, and control in an increasingly connected world.

*Chapter 8*

# Privacy-Focused Apps and Alternatives for a More Secure Mobile Experience

In today's digital environment, users often face a difficult choice between convenience and privacy. Many popular mobile applications offer powerful features, seamless integration, and personalized experiences, but these benefits frequently come at the cost of extensive data collection and user tracking. Fortunately, an increasing number of developers and organizations are creating privacy-focused alternatives designed to provide useful functionality while minimizing surveillance, advertising, profiling, and unnecessary data collection. Understanding how to identify and use privacy-focused apps can significantly improve your digital security and help you regain control over your personal information.

Privacy-focused applications are built around a fundamentally different philosophy than many mainstream services. Instead of maximizing data collection, these apps prioritize user confidentiality, transparency, security, and control. Their goal is to provide essential services while collecting as little personal information as possible. In many cases, privacy-focused developers adopt a principle known as data minimization, which means collecting only the information absolutely necessary for the app to function.

One of the first categories where privacy-focused alternatives have gained popularity is web browsing. Traditional browsers often collect browsing activity, synchronize data across devices, support advertising ecosystems, and allow various forms of tracking. Privacy-oriented browsers attempt to limit these practices by blocking trackers, preventing fingerprinting, enforcing encrypted connections, and reducing unnecessary data sharing. Using a privacy-focused browser can significantly reduce the amount of information advertisers and third parties collect about online activities.

Search engines represent another important area for privacy protection. Most mainstream search services collect queries, track user behavior, store search histories, and use collected information to personalize results and advertisements. Privacy-focused search engines aim to provide useful results without creating detailed profiles of users. They generally avoid storing personally identifiable information and minimize long-term tracking. While no search engine is entirely free from privacy considerations, some services prioritize confidentiality more effectively than others.

Messaging applications have become a central part of daily communication. Messages often contain personal conversations, business discussions, financial information, family matters, and sensitive details that users reasonably expect to remain private. Privacy-focused messaging apps frequently utilize end-to-end encryption, meaning messages can only be read by the intended sender and recipient. Even the service provider may be unable to access the contents of encrypted conversations. Understanding encryption and selecting secure communication platforms can dramatically improve privacy.

Email remains one of the most widely used communication technologies, yet many email providers analyze message contents for advertising, analytics, or service optimization purposes. Privacy-focused email services seek to reduce these concerns by emphasizing encryption, limited data collection, transparent policies, and user control. Selecting a privacy-conscious email provider can help protect sensitive communications and reduce exposure to tracking.

Cloud storage services offer convenience by allowing users to access files across multiple devices. However, cloud storage also introduces privacy concerns because personal documents, photos, videos, and other information are stored on remote servers. Privacy-focused cloud storage providers often use encryption methods that prevent even the service provider from viewing user content. These services emphasize confidentiality while still providing the convenience of remote access and synchronization.

Virtual private networks, commonly known as VPNs, have become increasingly popular among privacy-conscious users. A VPN encrypts internet traffic and routes it through secure servers, making it more difficult for third parties to monitor online activities. While VPNs are not a complete privacy solution, they provide valuable protection when using public Wi-Fi networks and can reduce certain forms of tracking. However, users should carefully evaluate VPN providers because privacy claims vary significantly across services.

Password managers represent another category of privacy-enhancing tools. Strong account security is essential for protecting personal information, and password managers help users generate and store unique credentials securely. Privacy-focused password managers often use strong encryption techniques that ensure only the user can access stored passwords. By reducing password reuse and strengthening authentication practices, password managers contribute significantly to overall security.

Note-taking applications may seem harmless, but they often contain highly sensitive information. Users frequently store personal reminders, business plans, financial notes, medical details, passwords, and confidential ideas within digital note systems. Privacy-focused note-taking apps emphasize encryption, local storage options, and limited data collection. These features help ensure that personal information remains private.

Photo storage and sharing services present additional privacy considerations. Modern smartphones contain thousands of personal photographs documenting family events, travel experiences, social relationships, and everyday activities. Privacy-focused photo applications often provide stronger encryption, reduced metadata collection, and greater control over sharing options. Some services even allow users to remove location information and other identifying details before sharing images.

Calendar applications also deserve attention from a privacy perspective. Calendars often contain detailed information about appointments, travel plans, work schedules, medical visits, and personal routines. Privacy-conscious calendar services aim to protect this information through encryption and limited data collection. Given the sensitive nature of scheduling information, selecting trustworthy calendar tools can improve overall privacy.

One of the defining characteristics of privacy-focused applications is transparency. Many privacy-oriented developers publish clear privacy policies, open-source code, security audits, and detailed explanations of data practices. Transparency allows users and independent researchers to verify security claims rather than relying solely on marketing materials. Open-source software is particularly valuable because experts can inspect the code for vulnerabilities, hidden tracking mechanisms, and other concerns.

Another important concept is decentralization. Traditional services often store data in centralized systems controlled by a single organization. Decentralized platforms distribute information across multiple systems or allow users greater control over storage. While decentralization introduces certain complexities, it can reduce the risks associated with centralized data collection and large-scale breaches.

Privacy-focused apps often challenge the assumption that extensive data collection is necessary for modern technology. Many developers have demonstrated that useful, innovative, and competitive services can operate successfully while respecting user privacy. These examples encourage broader discussions about ethical technology design and responsible data practices.

Users should understand that no application provides perfect privacy. Every digital service involves some level of trust, risk, and tradeoff. Privacy-focused tools reduce risks but do not eliminate them entirely. Effective privacy protection requires a combination of secure applications, informed decision-making, strong passwords, updated software, cautious behavior, and ongoing awareness.

One common misconception is that privacy-focused apps are only for highly technical users or individuals with something to hide. In reality, privacy benefits everyone. Personal information can be misused for identity theft, fraud, manipulation, discrimination, surveillance, and other harmful purposes. Protecting privacy is simply a form of responsible digital self-defense.

When evaluating privacy-focused alternatives, users should consider several factors. These include the developer's reputation, privacy policy transparency, security features, encryption practices, data collection policies, business model, and independent security reviews. Taking time to research applications before adoption can prevent future problems and support more informed choices.

Privacy-focused ecosystems are expanding rapidly. As public awareness grows, developers continue introducing innovative tools that balance convenience and confidentiality. This trend benefits users by increasing competition and encouraging stronger privacy protections across the technology industry.

Ultimately, adopting privacy-focused apps is not about rejecting technology. It is about choosing technologies that align with personal values and security goals. Every application installed on a smartphone represents a relationship between the user and the developer. By supporting organizations that prioritize privacy, users encourage responsible innovation while protecting their own information.

The future of mobile privacy will likely depend on both technological advancements and consumer choices. Users who understand privacy-focused alternatives are better equipped to navigate the digital landscape, reduce unnecessary exposure, and maintain greater control over their personal information. Through thoughtful app selection and informed decision-making, individuals can enjoy the benefits of modern technology without surrendering more privacy than necessary.

### *Olivia rarely considered privacy beyond basic passwords*

Olivia considered herself a practical person. As a financial consultant, she spent much of her day communicating with clients, reviewing documents, scheduling meetings, and managing sensitive information. Her smartphone served as an essential business tool, and she depended on numerous applications to remain productive.

For years, Olivia rarely considered privacy beyond basic passwords and software updates. Like most people, she used whatever apps were most popular. Convenience mattered far more than data collection practices. If an application worked well, she used it without much thought.

Everything changed during a cybersecurity seminar hosted by a professional association. One of the speakers discussed privacy-focused technology and demonstrated how many popular apps collected extensive information about users. The presentation included examples of tracking systems, advertising networks, behavioral profiling, and data-sharing arrangements.

Olivia was surprised by the scale of the collection. She had always assumed that some data gathering occurred, but she had never realized how extensive it could be.

After the seminar, she decided to conduct an experiment. Rather than accepting default technology choices, she would explore privacy-focused alternatives and evaluate whether they could meet her professional needs.

She started with her web browser. The browser she had used for years synchronized activity across devices and provided personalized recommendations. However, it also collected significant behavioral information. Olivia researched privacy-oriented alternatives and selected one known for tracker blocking and enhanced security features.

The transition was smoother than expected. Websites loaded normally, online banking functioned properly, and her productivity remained unchanged. Yet she gained additional protections against tracking and fingerprinting.

Encouraged by the experience, Olivia examined other areas of her digital life. She explored encrypted messaging applications, privacy-focused email providers, and secure cloud storage services. While some changes required minor adjustments, most alternatives provided familiar functionality with stronger privacy protections.

One of the most significant improvements involved messaging. Olivia frequently discussed sensitive financial matters with clients. After learning more about end-to-end encryption, she encouraged several clients to use secure communication channels for confidential conversations. The change improved both privacy and professional confidence.

As weeks turned into months, Olivia continued refining her digital environment. She replaced several applications that collected excessive information and began prioritizing developers with transparent privacy practices. Her decisions were not driven by fear but by a desire for greater control.

During this process, she encountered resistance from some colleagues. A few argued that privacy concerns were exaggerated. Others believed that switching applications created unnecessary inconvenience.

Rather than debating, Olivia focused on practical outcomes. She explained that privacy-focused tools often provided similar functionality while reducing data exposure. The goal was not secrecy but responsible information management.

One colleague, Michael, became particularly interested after hearing Olivia describe her experiences. He worked in healthcare and regularly handled confidential patient information. Inspired by Olivia's approach, he began evaluating his own technology choices.

Several months later, Michael thanked her for introducing the concept. He had adopted several privacy-focused tools and felt more confident about protecting sensitive communications. The conversation reinforced Olivia's belief that awareness could create meaningful change.

As her understanding deepened, Olivia noticed an unexpected benefit. She became more intentional about technology in general. Rather than automatically downloading popular apps, she evaluated developers, reviewed privacy policies, and considered business models. This mindset extended beyond privacy and improved her overall cybersecurity awareness.

One afternoon, Olivia attended another industry conference. During a networking session, participants discussed data breaches affecting major organizations. Many attendees expressed frustration about the frequency of incidents and the amount of personal information exposed.

Listening to the conversation, Olivia realized how much her perspective had evolved. She understood that no technology could eliminate all risks. However, she also recognized that users possessed more influence than they often realized. Every application choice represented a decision about trust, data sharing, and privacy.

Over time, Olivia built a personal technology ecosystem centered on security, transparency, and control. She still used modern tools, cloud services, messaging platforms, and mobile applications. The difference was that she selected them more carefully and understood the tradeoffs involved.

Her smartphone remained just as useful as before. In many ways, it became even more valuable because she trusted it more. She knew where her information was stored, how it was protected, and which organizations had access to it.

Looking back, Olivia appreciated how a single seminar had sparked a journey of discovery. What began as curiosity evolved into a broader understanding of digital privacy and responsible technology use.

Most importantly, she learned that privacy-focused apps were not about restricting possibilities. They were about expanding choices. Instead of accepting whatever options were most heavily marketed, users could choose services that aligned with their own priorities and values.

That realization became one of the most empowering lessons of her career. Technology should serve users, not the other way around. By selecting tools thoughtfully and supporting developers who respected privacy, individuals could shape a digital environment that balanced convenience, functionality, and security.

As new technologies emerged and the digital world continued evolving, Olivia remained confident in her approach. Trends would change, platforms would rise and fall, and new challenges would appear. Yet the principles she had learned—awareness, transparency, control, and informed decision-making—would remain relevant.

Her experience demonstrated a simple truth: privacy is not achieved through a single application or setting. It is built through a series of thoughtful choices made consistently over time. Each choice contributes to a safer, more secure, and more empowering digital experience.

By embracing privacy-focused alternatives and understanding how technology handles personal information, Olivia had taken meaningful steps toward protecting what mattered most. In an increasingly connected world, that knowledge proved to be one of the most valuable assets she possessed.

Protecting your privacy is not a one-time task. Many people mistakenly believe that privacy can be achieved simply by changing a few settings, installing a security app, or deleting a handful of risky applications. While these actions are valuable, true privacy protection requires a long-term strategy. The digital world is constantly evolving. New applications are released every day, operating systems receive updates, cybercriminals develop new attack methods, and companies continuously create new ways to collect and analyze user data. To remain protected, individuals must adopt a privacy mindset that becomes part of their everyday digital habits.

A long-term privacy strategy begins with understanding that personal information has value. Many companies view data as a business asset. Information about user behavior, purchasing habits, locations, interests, relationships, and online activities can be used for advertising, analytics, personalization and profit generation. Cybercriminals view the same information as an opportunity to identify theft, financial fraud, account compromise, and social engineering attacks. Recognizing the

*Chapter 9*

# Building a Long-Term Mobile Privacy Strategy

Protecting your privacy is not a one-time task. Many people mistakenly believe that privacy can be achieved simply by changing a few settings, installing a security app, or deleting a handful of risky applications. While those actions are valuable, true privacy protection requires a long-term strategy. The digital world is constantly evolving. New applications are released every day, operating systems receive updates, cybercriminals develop new attack methods, and companies continuously create new ways to collect and analyze user data. To remain protected, individuals must adopt a privacy mindset that becomes part of their daily digital habits.

A long-term privacy strategy begins with understanding that personal information has value. Many companies view data as a business asset. Information about user behavior, purchasing habits, locations, interests, relationships, and online activities can be used for advertising, analytics, personalization, and profit generation. Cybercriminals view the same information as an opportunity for identity theft, financial fraud, account compromise, and social engineering attacks. Recognizing the value of personal information helps users understand why privacy deserves ongoing attention.

The first component of a long-term privacy strategy is awareness. Awareness means understanding how technology works, recognizing privacy risks, and staying informed about emerging threats. Users do not need to become cybersecurity experts, but they should maintain a basic understanding of the technologies they use every day. Reading technology news, reviewing privacy updates, and learning about new security features can help users make informed decisions and adapt to changing circumstances.

The second component is intentionality. Many privacy problems arise because users make decisions automatically without considering the consequences. They install apps quickly, approve permissions without review, accept default settings, and share information without evaluating the risks. Intentional users pause before making decisions. They ask questions such as: Why is this information being requested? Is this permission necessary? Do I trust this developer? What information am I sharing? These simple questions create a powerful foundation for privacy protection.

Account management represents another critical aspect of a long-term strategy. Every online account contains personal information that may become a target for cybercriminals. Users should regularly review account security settings, update passwords, enable multi-factor authentication, and remove accounts they no longer use. Forgotten accounts often contain outdated information and may become vulnerable if neglected. Periodic account audits help reduce unnecessary exposure.

Application management should also become a routine practice. Smartphones often accumulate dozens or even hundreds of apps over time. Some are used frequently, while others are forgotten shortly after installation. Every installed app represents a potential source of data collection and security risk. Reviewing installed applications regularly allows users to remove unnecessary software, revoke permissions, and reduce the overall attack surface of their devices.

Privacy-conscious users should establish a habit of reviewing permissions periodically. Permissions that seemed reasonable months ago may no longer be necessary. New app updates may introduce additional functionality and request expanded access. Regular permission reviews ensure that applications maintain only the access they genuinely require.

Data minimization remains one of the most effective privacy principles. The less information shared, the less information that can be exposed, stolen, misused, or analyzed. Users should avoid providing unnecessary details when creating accounts, completing profiles, or participating in online services. Not every platform needs a phone number, physical address, birth date, or extensive personal information. Limiting disclosure reduces privacy risks significantly.

Device maintenance is another essential component of long-term privacy protection. Smartphones should be updated regularly to ensure security vulnerabilities are patched promptly. Outdated operating systems and applications often contain weaknesses that attackers actively exploit. Automatic updates can simplify this process and help users remain protected without constant monitoring.

Backup strategies are often overlooked in privacy discussions, yet they play an important role. Data loss can occur through device failures, theft, malware infections, accidental deletion, or account compromise. Secure backups allow users to recover important information without relying entirely on service providers. Backups should themselves be protected through encryption and secure storage practices.

Privacy and security are closely related but distinct concepts. Security focuses on protecting information from unauthorized access, while privacy focuses on controlling how information is collected, used, and shared. A comprehensive strategy must address both areas simultaneously. Strong security measures help prevent unauthorized access, while thoughtful privacy practices reduce unnecessary data exposure.

Users should also recognize the importance of physical device security. Smartphones often contain access to banking accounts, emails, business systems, personal photos, healthcare information, and social media profiles. Strong screen locks, biometric authentication, automatic locking features, and remote wipe capabilities help protect devices if they are lost or stolen. Physical access often leads directly to privacy risks.

Family privacy planning deserves special consideration. Many households share devices, accounts, cloud storage systems, and communication platforms. Parents should teach children about privacy principles, safe app usage, and responsible information sharing. Establishing healthy digital habits early helps younger users develop stronger privacy awareness as technology becomes increasingly integrated into daily life.

Social media requires ongoing attention as well. Information shared publicly today may remain accessible for years. Photos, comments, location tags, and personal details can reveal far more than intended. Users should periodically review social media profiles, privacy settings, friend lists, and historical content. Managing digital footprints is an ongoing process rather than a one-time adjustment.

One valuable habit involves conducting annual privacy audits. During a privacy audit, users systematically review accounts, apps, permissions, devices, cloud storage services, social media profiles, and security settings. This process helps identify outdated configurations, unnecessary accounts, excessive permissions, and new opportunities for improvement. Annual reviews provide a structured approach to maintaining privacy over time.

Another important principle is adaptability. Privacy threats evolve continuously. New technologies such as artificial intelligence, wearable devices, smart homes, connected vehicles, augmented reality systems, and digital assistants create new opportunities for data collection. Users who remain adaptable can adjust their strategies as technology changes.

Organizations and governments also influence privacy landscapes through regulations, policies, and technology standards. Understanding major privacy developments helps users make informed choices regarding services, platforms, and digital rights. Knowledge empowers users to advocate for stronger protections and support organizations that prioritize privacy.

Privacy should not be viewed as an obstacle to innovation. Rather, it should be considered a component of responsible technology use. Users can enjoy modern applications, online services, and digital conveniences while still maintaining meaningful control over personal information. The goal is balance, not isolation.

A successful long-term privacy strategy ultimately becomes a habit rather than a project. Small actions performed consistently often provide greater protection than occasional major efforts. Reviewing permissions, updating software, managing accounts, evaluating apps, and staying informed require relatively little time when incorporated into regular routines.

The most privacy-conscious individuals understand that perfection is neither realistic nor necessary. Privacy protection is about reducing risk, increasing awareness, and maintaining control. Every thoughtful decision contributes to a stronger privacy posture. Over time, these decisions accumulate into a comprehensive strategy capable of adapting to an ever-changing digital world.

By building a long-term privacy strategy, users move beyond reactive security measures and develop proactive habits that support ongoing protection. Technology will continue evolving, but the principles of awareness, intentionality, control, and responsibility will remain valuable regardless of future innovations. These principles provide a foundation for navigating the digital future with confidence and resilience.

### *James had spent years accumulating digital assets*

James had always considered himself reasonably careful with technology. He used strong passwords, avoided suspicious emails, and updated his smartphone occasionally. Yet privacy was never something he thought about consistently. Like many people, he approached security reactively. When a problem appeared, he addressed it. Otherwise, he focused on more immediate concerns.

That mindset changed after a conversation with his daughter, Emily.

Emily was studying information systems at a local university and often discussed cybersecurity topics at family dinners. One evening, she asked her father a simple question.

"Dad, when was the last time you reviewed your privacy settings?"

James laughed.

"I honestly have no idea."

Emily smiled.

"That's exactly why privacy problems happen."

The conversation sparked James's curiosity. Over the following weeks, he began examining his digital habits more closely. What started as a simple review of privacy settings evolved into a broader understanding of how much information accumulated across his devices and accounts.

He discovered old social media profiles he had forgotten existed. Several online accounts contained outdated information. Dozens of unused applications remained installed on his smartphone. Some still possessed permissions he no longer remembered granting.

The discoveries were not alarming, but they highlighted a pattern. James had spent years accumulating digital assets without maintaining them.

Rather than trying to solve everything at once, he adopted a systematic approach. Each weekend, he focused on one area. One week he reviewed passwords. Another week he examined permissions. Later, he organized cloud storage accounts and removed unused applications.

The gradual approach proved effective. Small improvements accumulated over time without becoming overwhelming.

Several months later, James noticed meaningful changes. His smartphone contained fewer apps, fewer notifications, and fewer unnecessary permissions. Account security was stronger. Privacy settings were configured intentionally rather than left at defaults. Most importantly, he understood his digital environment far better than before.

The benefits extended beyond technology. James felt more organized and more in control. Instead of wondering how information was being handled, he possessed a clearer understanding of the systems he relied upon daily.

One afternoon, a coworker named Robert mentioned concerns about identity theft after receiving a notification about a data breach. The conversation reminded James of his own journey. Rather than focusing solely on the breach itself, he explained the importance of ongoing privacy management.

"A lot of people treat privacy like a one-time task," James said. "But it's more like maintaining a house. You don't fix everything once and forget about it."

Robert appreciated the analogy. He later adopted several of the habits James described, including regular account reviews and permission audits.

As time passed, privacy management became part of James's routine. At the beginning of each month, he reviewed account activity. Every few months, he examined installed apps and permissions. Once a year, he conducted a more comprehensive privacy audit.

The process required surprisingly little effort because it had become habitual.

Meanwhile, technology continued evolving. New devices entered the market. Artificial intelligence tools became more common. Applications introduced new features and capabilities. Yet James no longer felt overwhelmed by change.

Instead, he applied the same principles consistently. Understand the technology. Evaluate the risks. Make informed decisions. Review settings regularly. Maintain control.

These habits provided stability even as the digital landscape shifted around him.

One particularly valuable lesson involved family education. James began discussing privacy topics with his children and grandchildren. Rather than focusing on fear or worst-case scenarios, he emphasized awareness and responsibility. The conversations helped younger family members develop healthy digital habits early in life.

Years later, James reflected on how much his perspective had changed. Privacy was no longer something he thought about only after hearing news about a breach or scam. It had become an ordinary part of responsible technology use.

He still enjoyed social media, online shopping, cloud services, streaming platforms, and mobile apps. The difference was that he engaged with them intentionally. Technology served his needs rather than operating without his awareness.

One evening, while reviewing his annual privacy checklist, James realized how many small actions had contributed to his overall protection. No single setting or application had transformed his privacy. Instead, the improvement resulted from consistent habits practiced over time.

That realization reinforced one of the most important lessons he had learned. Privacy is rarely lost through a single event, and it is rarely protected through a single action. Both outcomes result from countless small decisions made every day.

By choosing awareness over convenience, intentionality over automation, and responsibility over neglect, James had built a privacy strategy capable of adapting to an ever-changing digital world.

His journey demonstrated that long-term privacy is not reserved for cybersecurity experts or technology enthusiasts. It is achievable for anyone willing to develop thoughtful habits and remain engaged with the technologies they use.

As new innovations continued shaping the future, James felt confident in his ability to adapt. He knew challenges would emerge, but he also understood that the principles guiding his decisions would remain relevant.

Privacy was no longer a destination he hoped to reach. It had become a continuous practice—one that strengthened with every informed choice he made. Through consistency, awareness, and deliberate action, he had transformed privacy from an abstract concept into a practical part of everyday life.

And in a world increasingly driven by data, that transformation proved to be one of the most valuable investments he could make.

*Chapter 10*

# Creating Your Personal Mobile Privacy Action Plan

Throughout this book, you have explored the foundations of mobile privacy, app permissions, tracking technologies, privacy policies, authentication systems, malicious applications, privacy settings, privacy-focused alternatives, and long-term privacy strategies. Knowledge is powerful, but knowledge alone does not create protection. Real privacy improvements occur when information is transformed into action. The purpose of this final chapter is to help you create a practical, personalized mobile privacy action plan that you can implement immediately and maintain over time.

Many users become overwhelmed when learning about privacy risks. They discover the extent of data collection, tracking technologies, advertising networks, and cyber threats, and they begin to believe that privacy is impossible. In reality, privacy protection is not about eliminating all risk. It is about reducing unnecessary exposure, increasing control, and making informed decisions. A well-designed privacy action plan provides structure and clarity, allowing users to improve privacy gradually without feeling overwhelmed.

The first step in creating a privacy action plan is conducting a personal privacy assessment. Before making changes, users should evaluate their current situation. How many apps are installed on the device? Which permissions have been granted? How many online accounts exist? Are strong passwords being used? Is multi-factor authentication enabled? What information is shared publicly on social media? The answers to these questions provide a baseline from which improvements can be measured.

A privacy assessment should begin with device security. Users should verify that smartphones are protected with strong screen locks. Biometric authentication, passcodes, or complex passwords should be enabled whenever possible. Automatic locking features should be configured to activate after short periods of inactivity. Remote device location and remote wipe capabilities should also be enabled in case the device is lost or stolen.

The second step involves reviewing installed applications. Most smartphones contain apps that are rarely used or completely forgotten. Each application represents a potential source of data collection and a possible security risk. Users should systematically evaluate every installed app and ask a simple question: Do I still need this? Unnecessary applications should be removed. Reducing the number of installed apps reduces the overall attack surface and limits opportunities for unnecessary data collection.

After removing unused apps, attention should shift to permissions. Permission audits are among the most effective privacy improvements available. Users should examine permissions granted to each application and determine whether they remain necessary. Location access, microphone permissions, camera permissions, contacts access, storage permissions, and other sensitive privileges should be reviewed carefully. Applications should receive only the access required to perform their intended functions.

Account security represents the next critical area. Users should identify their most important accounts, including email services, banking platforms, cloud storage providers, healthcare portals, social media accounts, and work-related systems. Strong, unique passwords should be used for each account. Multi-factor authentication should be enabled wherever available. Password managers can simplify this process while improving security significantly.

Email accounts deserve particular attention because they often serve as recovery mechanisms for other services. If an attacker gains access to a primary email account, they may be able to reset passwords and compromise numerous connected accounts. Securing email accounts should therefore be considered a top priority within any privacy action plan.

The next step involves evaluating social media privacy. Social platforms frequently contain large amounts of personal information. Users should review profile visibility settings, audience controls, location sharing options, friend lists, tagging permissions, advertising preferences, and historical content. Information that no longer serves a purpose or creates unnecessary exposure should be removed or restricted.

Location privacy should also be addressed systematically. Users should identify which apps genuinely require location access and which do not. For most applications, limiting access to "While Using the App" provides an excellent balance between convenience and privacy. Continuous background tracking should be reserved only for apps with legitimate operational needs.

Advertising and tracking controls provide another opportunity for improvement. Both Android and iOS offer settings that allow users to limit personalized advertising and restrict tracking activities. Many applications also include individual privacy controls that reduce data sharing and behavioral profiling. Reviewing these settings can significantly decrease unnecessary tracking.

Data backup planning should be incorporated into every privacy strategy. Important information should be backed up regularly using secure methods. Backups protect against device failures, malware infections, accidental deletions, and account compromises. Whenever possible, backups should be encrypted to ensure confidentiality.

Users should also establish a software update routine. Operating systems and applications release updates frequently to address security vulnerabilities and improve privacy protections. Automatic updates can simplify this process and ensure that devices remain protected against known threats.

A strong privacy action plan includes ongoing education. Technology changes rapidly, and new privacy challenges emerge continuously. Users should commit to staying informed about major developments affecting mobile security and privacy. This does not require constant monitoring, but periodic learning helps maintain awareness and adaptability.

One useful approach involves creating a monthly privacy checklist. The checklist may include reviewing account activity, checking permissions, updating software, examining installed applications, monitoring privacy settings, and reviewing security alerts. Monthly reviews require little time but provide substantial long-term benefits.

Quarterly reviews can address broader issues. Every three months, users may conduct deeper evaluations of account security, social media settings, cloud storage practices, backup systems, and privacy policies. These reviews help ensure that privacy measures remain effective as technologies evolve.

Annual privacy audits provide an opportunity for comprehensive evaluation. During an annual audit, users can review every major component of their digital lives, identify areas for improvement, and update privacy goals. This structured approach transforms privacy management into an ongoing process rather than an occasional reaction to news headlines or security incidents.

Privacy goals should be realistic and personalized. Not every user requires the same level of protection. A journalist, healthcare professional, business executive, student, retiree, and small business owner may all face different privacy considerations. The most effective action plans reflect individual circumstances, risk levels, and personal preferences.

Users should remember that privacy and convenience often exist on a spectrum. Some privacy-enhancing measures may introduce minor inconveniences. The goal is not to maximize privacy at all costs but to find a balance that aligns with personal priorities. Thoughtful compromises often produce the most sustainable results.

Another important principle is consistency. Small actions performed regularly are more effective than major efforts performed once and forgotten. Reviewing permissions, updating software, monitoring accounts, and staying informed require relatively little time when integrated into normal routines. Consistency transforms privacy protection from a project into a habit.

Perhaps the most important aspect of any privacy action plan is mindset. Privacy should not be driven by fear, paranoia, or distrust. Instead, it should be viewed as a form of responsible digital stewardship. Just as individuals protect physical property, financial assets, and personal relationships, they should also protect personal information.

The digital world offers extraordinary opportunities for communication, education, entertainment, business, healthcare, and personal growth. Privacy protection does not require rejecting these benefits. Rather, it involves using technology thoughtfully and maintaining control over how personal information is collected, shared, and used.

As you conclude this book, remember that privacy is not a destination. It is a continuous process of awareness, evaluation, and improvement. Every permission reviewed, account secured, setting adjusted, and informed decision made contributes to a stronger privacy posture. The action plan you create today will serve as a foundation for protecting your information in an increasingly connected world.

The knowledge you have gained throughout this book provides the tools. Your decisions and actions will determine the results. By applying these principles consistently, you can enjoy the advantages of modern technology while maintaining meaningful control over your personal information, digital identity, and privacy for years to come.

### *Nathan continued refining his strategy*

Nathan had always considered himself an ordinary smartphone user. He used mobile banking apps, social media platforms, messaging services, streaming applications, shopping websites, and productivity tools just like millions of other people. Technology made life easier, and for years he rarely thought about privacy beyond choosing passwords and updating software occasionally.

That changed after attending a community technology workshop.

The workshop focused on mobile privacy and app security. Over several hours, participants learned about permissions, tracking technologies, malicious apps, data collection practices, account protection, and privacy settings. Nathan found the information fascinating but also somewhat overwhelming.

By the end of the workshop, he realized how much information his smartphone generated and how many opportunities existed to improve privacy. However, he also felt uncertain about where to begin.

As he drove home, one message from the instructor remained in his mind.

"Don't try to fix everything at once. Create a plan."

The following weekend, Nathan sat down with a notebook and decided to do exactly that.

He started by listing every major area of his digital life. Smartphone security. Apps. Passwords. Social media. Cloud storage. Email. Banking. Privacy settings. The list was longer than expected, but seeing everything organized helped reduce the feeling of being overwhelmed.

Next, he performed a simple assessment. How many apps were installed? Which permissions had been granted? Which accounts used multi-factor authentication? Which services contained sensitive information?

The answers surprised him.

Several apps had not been used in years. Numerous permissions remained enabled without clear justification. Some important accounts still relied solely on passwords. The discoveries were not alarming, but they highlighted opportunities for improvement.

Rather than attempting to address everything immediately, Nathan created a schedule.

Week one focused on applications. He removed unused software and reviewed permissions. Week two addressed passwords and authentication. Week three involved social media privacy settings. Week four covered backups and cloud storage.

The structured approach worked remarkably well.

Each task required only a small amount of time, yet meaningful improvements accumulated quickly. Within a month, his smartphone contained fewer apps, stronger account protections, and more carefully configured privacy settings.

Encouraged by the results, Nathan continued refining his strategy.

He created a monthly reminder to review permissions and account activity. Quarterly reminders focused on broader privacy reviews. Annual reminders scheduled comprehensive audits. What initially seemed complicated gradually became routine.

Several months later, a friend named Lucas mentioned concerns about a recent data breach affecting an online service they both used.

"How do you keep track of all this stuff?" Lucas asked.

Nathan smiled.

"I stopped trying to remember everything. I built a system."

He explained the checklist approach and the importance of small, consistent actions. Lucas appreciated the advice and began creating his own privacy plan.

Their conversation highlighted one of Nathan's most important discoveries. Privacy protection was not about technical expertise. It was about organization and consistency.

Over time, Nathan noticed another benefit. The more he understood his digital environment, the more confident he felt using technology. News stories about data breaches, scams, and tracking systems no longer created anxiety. Instead, they reinforced the importance of maintaining good habits.

One evening, while reviewing his monthly checklist, Nathan reflected on how much his perspective had changed.

Before the workshop, privacy had felt abstract and complicated. Now it felt practical and manageable. The difference was not the technology itself. The difference was having a plan.

He realized that most privacy failures occurred not because people lacked intelligence but because they lacked structure. Without a plan, important tasks were forgotten. Permissions accumulated. Accounts remained unsecured. Settings went unreviewed.

A plan transformed awareness into action.

Years passed, and technology continued evolving. New apps emerged. Devices became more sophisticated. Artificial intelligence systems became increasingly common. Yet Nathan's core approach remained effective because it focused on principles rather than specific technologies.

Review regularly. Limit unnecessary exposure. Secure important accounts. Stay informed. Adapt when needed.

These habits provided a stable foundation regardless of changing trends.

As his children grew older and began using smartphones of their own, Nathan shared the lessons he had learned. Rather than overwhelming them with technical details, he emphasized responsibility and awareness.

"Technology isn't the problem," he often said. "Not paying attention is."

The advice resonated because it was simple and practical.

Looking back, Nathan appreciated how a single workshop had influenced his approach to digital life. The information itself was valuable, but the real transformation occurred when he converted knowledge into action.

Privacy was no longer something he hoped to achieve someday. It had become part of his routine. A habit. A mindset.

Most importantly, he understood that perfection was unnecessary. Mistakes would happen. Technology would change. New risks would emerge. What mattered was maintaining awareness and continuing to improve over time.

His experience demonstrated the central lesson of this entire book: privacy is not created by one setting, one application, or one decision. It is built through countless small choices made consistently.

Every permission reviewed. Every password strengthened. Every app evaluated. Every setting adjusted. Every informed decision contributed to greater control and protection.

As Nathan completed another monthly review and set his phone aside for the evening, he felt a sense of confidence. Not because his privacy was perfect, but because he had developed the habits necessary to protect it.

In an increasingly connected world, those habits had become one of his most valuable assets.

And they would continue serving him well for years to come.

# Final Thoughts: Taking Control of Your Mobile Privacy Future

The journey through *App Protection and Privacy Mastery* has revealed an important truth about modern technology: privacy is not something that is automatically provided, nor is it something that disappears overnight. Privacy exists on a spectrum of awareness, responsibility, and intentional action. Every day, billions of people interact with mobile applications without fully understanding how much information is being collected, analyzed, stored, shared, and monetized. Yet the goal of this book has never been to create fear or distrust. Instead, it has been to provide knowledge, practical tools, and confidence so that you can make informed decisions about your digital life.

As smartphones have evolved into powerful personal assistants, entertainment centers, communication hubs, financial tools, and business platforms, they have also become repositories of some of the most sensitive information people possess. Mobile devices contain photographs, videos, contacts, financial records, passwords, health information, travel histories, personal conversations, and countless other details that reveal who we are and how we live. Protecting this information is no longer optional. It has become an essential component of modern life.

One of the most valuable lessons from this book is that privacy begins with awareness. Many people unknowingly surrender personal information simply because they are unaware of how technology operates. They install applications without reviewing permissions, accept default settings without question, and provide information without considering how it might be used. Awareness transforms passive users into informed decision-makers. Once you understand how apps collect data, track behavior, request permissions, and share information, you gain the ability to make choices rather than simply accepting whatever technology companies decide for you.

Another important lesson is that privacy is not about hiding. One of the most common misconceptions is that only people with something to hide care about privacy. In reality, privacy is about maintaining control over personal information. Most people lock their homes, protect their financial accounts, and safeguard personal records not because they are doing anything wrong, but because they value security and autonomy. Digital privacy follows the same principle. Protecting information is a normal and responsible part of modern life.

Throughout this book, you have learned that every permission granted to an app creates a pathway for information to flow. Some permissions are necessary and support valuable functionality. Others may be excessive or unnecessary. By reviewing permissions carefully and limiting access to only what is required, users can significantly reduce their exposure without sacrificing convenience. Small actions such as limiting location access, restricting microphone permissions, or reviewing contact sharing settings often provide meaningful privacy benefits.

You have also explored how tracking technologies operate behind the scenes. Many users are surprised to discover the extent to which advertising networks, analytics systems, and third-party services monitor behavior across apps and platforms. Yet understanding these systems is empowering. Once you recognize how tracking works, you can begin limiting unnecessary exposure through privacy settings, app selection, and informed usage habits. Knowledge transforms invisible processes into manageable risks.

The role of privacy policies has been another important topic. While privacy policies are often lengthy and difficult to read, they remain valuable sources of information. Learning to identify key sections and recognize warning signs allows users to evaluate applications more effectively. Trust should never be based solely on marketing materials or popularity. Transparency, accountability, and clear communication are important indicators of responsible data practices.

Strong authentication and account security form another critical layer of privacy protection. Passwords, multi-factor authentication, password managers, and account monitoring systems help ensure that personal information remains accessible only to authorized users. Many privacy breaches occur not because applications are inherently unsafe but because accounts become compromised through weak passwords, phishing attacks, or credential reuse. Strengthening account security remains one of the most effective actions users can take.

The threat posed by malicious applications, fake apps, spyware, and mobile scams highlights the importance of caution and critical thinking. Cybercriminals often rely on deception rather than technical sophistication. They exploit trust, urgency, curiosity, and convenience to achieve their objectives. Users who develop healthy skepticism and verify information before acting become far less likely to fall victim to these attacks.

Privacy settings provide another powerful opportunity for protection. Many applications offer extensive controls that allow users to customize how information is collected, shared, and displayed. Unfortunately, these settings often remain hidden or overlooked. Taking time to review privacy options can significantly improve control over personal information. In many cases, meaningful privacy improvements can be achieved in just a few minutes.

Privacy-focused applications and services demonstrate that extensive data collection is not the only viable business model. Developers around the world are creating tools that prioritize confidentiality, transparency, and user control. Supporting these alternatives encourages responsible innovation while providing users with meaningful choices. Every app installed represents a relationship between the user and the developer. Choosing privacy-conscious providers helps shape the future of the technology industry.

Long-term privacy protection ultimately depends on habits rather than isolated actions. Technology changes continuously. New apps emerge, operating systems evolve, artificial intelligence becomes more sophisticated, and data collection methods become increasingly advanced. Users who adopt privacy-conscious habits are better equipped to adapt to these changes. Reviewing permissions, updating software, monitoring accounts, evaluating apps, and staying informed are simple practices that provide lasting benefits.

One of the most important themes throughout this book is balance. Privacy does not require abandoning technology, disconnecting from society, or eliminating convenience. Modern technology offers extraordinary benefits that improve communication, education, healthcare, entertainment, business, and personal productivity. The goal is not to reject these benefits but to use them responsibly. Privacy and convenience can coexist when users understand the tradeoffs involved and make intentional decisions.

As artificial intelligence, wearable devices, smart homes, connected vehicles, augmented reality systems, and other emerging technologies become more common, privacy challenges will continue evolving. The specific technologies may change, but the underlying principles will remain the same. Awareness, intentionality, transparency, control, and responsibility will continue serving as the foundation of effective privacy protection.

Perhaps the greatest lesson from this book is that privacy is ultimately about empowerment. Many people feel powerless when confronted with large technology companies, sophisticated tracking systems, and complex digital ecosystems. Yet users possess far more influence than they often realize. Every app installed, permission granted, setting adjusted, account secured, and service selected represents a choice. These choices shape digital experiences and determine how personal information is handled.

You do not need to implement every recommendation immediately. Privacy is a journey rather than a destination. Start with small improvements. Review permissions. Strengthen passwords. Enable multi-factor authentication. Remove unused applications. Explore privacy settings. Learn about the technologies you use most frequently. Over time, these actions accumulate into meaningful protection.

The digital world will continue expanding and becoming more interconnected. Mobile devices will remain central to daily life. New opportunities and new risks will emerge side by side. By applying the principles presented throughout this book, you can approach this future with confidence rather than uncertainty. You can enjoy the benefits of modern technology while maintaining meaningful control over your personal information.

Your privacy belongs to you. Your data has value. Your choices matter. The knowledge you have gained provides the foundation. The habits you develop will determine the results. As you move forward, remember that every informed decision contributes to a safer, more secure, and more private digital future.

Thank you for investing your time in learning about app protection and privacy mastery. May the lessons from this book help you navigate the digital world with confidence, awareness, and control for many years to come.

www.ingramcontent.com/pod-product-compliance
Lightning Source LLC
LaVergne TN
LVHW040519210926
848480LV00007BA/1523